DISPATCHING GOLIATH

Michael W. Bryant, Sr.

NSB

Next Step Books

Published by Next Step Books, P.O. Box 4563, Frankfort, KY 40604-4563. The views expressed by the author are not necessarily those of the publisher.

Cover and Interior Design by Virginia Smith

ISBN: 978-1-937671-63-1

GLORY TO GOD

"To God be glory forever and forever"
Galatians 1:5

First and foremost, this book is dedicated to God.
Without Him and the leadership of His Holy Spirit
this work would have never been written.
To Him I give all praise and glory!

In Memoriam

In honor of my wife Carol Lorraine Owens Bryant, who went to Heaven February 15, 2023, at age 77.

You are greatly missed. Our marriage of 57 years was the happiest time of my life.

Thank you for being the best soulmate, mom, and momo anyone could ask for.

You were our anchor, our center, our balance. We will always grieve your absence, and we will love you always and forever.

This book, along with many other things in my life, would not have been possible without you. As a Proverbs 31 woman you stood beside me through thick and thin, better or worse, richer or poorer.

I cannot talk about my life without having you

in my mind and heart.

All of us rejoice at your homegoing to be with Jesus. We look forward to being reunited with you.

You were the most beautiful woman I have ever known (inside and out).

God's presence, the memories, your pictures, visits to the cemetery and decorating your grave all help me to process you no longer being here and to keep going. I will not miss or grieve for you any less until I join you in Heaven. Thank you for being in my life. Thank you for being a wonderful wife and for giving me so much happiness.

As the song "Goodbye" written by Lionel Richie and performed by Kenny Rogers expresses, I wanted you for life, the two of us together, and never thought our story would end. It is not easy to say goodbye. But as the song says, there is peace where you are, and you are *always* in my heart.

Alfred Lloyd Tennyson wrote, "Tis better to loved and lost than never to have loved at all."

Thank You

To My Family

I wish I could find the words to express my love and appreciation for our family. Your mom and I called the four of you our trophies. The Lord blessed us beyond measure. God, in His creative genius gave you all life and your mom gave you birth. I am thankful that the Lord allowed me to your dad. All of you are the truest blessing of our lives. Life without you all is just incomprehensible. I think my decision to include the names of our children and grandchildren on our cemetery monument was an appropriate one. Since I already mentioned them by name in the book, I won't do it here. The gift of 4 kids, 12 grandkids (and spouses), plus so far one great grandson and one great granddaughter is like the proverbial gold at the end of the rainbow. Your mom and I will love you all forever! Thank you for loving us, respecting us, and caring for us.

To Others

Two people have played a part in getting this book published: William F. Carman, author of *Fishing with Daniel Boone: Fly Fishing the Streams of an American Hero* and others; and Virginia Smith, author of *The Woman Warrior: Deborah's Story* and others. Thank you for your help.

TABLE OF CONTENTS

Introduction

Charles Spurgeon said, "Visit many good books, but live in the Bible." No biblically based book should subtract from the Word of God but rather complement it. That's what I hope I have done with *Dispatching Goliath*. The work I have undertaken here has been birthed by God and guided by the leadership of the Holy Spirit. Over my years of preaching the gospel folks would sometimes compliment my sermons. Consistently I would respond with "The good stuff was the Lord's and any mistakes were mine." That is my heart in sharing this book. I have tried my best with God's help to carefully and humbly write what I feel the Lord wanted me to write. More than forty years ago people would occasionally ask me to consider writing a book. I appreciated their confidence in me to under-take such a task. I was interested but was so busy back then. I did get close. I wrote a dissertation of 187 pages as part of the requirement for my doctor-ate. Although never intended to be published, I guess it sort of purports to be a "book." I ap-proached the project of *Dispatching Goliath* with hu-mility and a heavy dependence on God. It is some-thing I earnestly prayed over. I began the writing without knowing what all the chapters would be about. While there are millions of books that have been published, each book is unique. The frustra-tion that I experienced took on various forms. Phys-ically it was hard. Having daily back pain (back sur-gery a few years ago) made it difficult to sit in front of the laptop. Screen time was difficult because of diminished vision and burning eyes. Turning eighty shortly after completing the work didn't help. Memory not that great at my age. Trying to harness my thoughts was also challenging. I would awake during the night with all these thoughts run-ning through my computer called the brain. Throughout the project there existed the concern that I would not be able to harness the information for the book that I wanted to include. I suspect that I will look back and think of certain Scriptures and/or illustrations that maybe I should have incorporated in my composition. I did explain in the book that my writing was not intended to use every biblical verse available for every topic. So, as you read what I have provided you may be thinking another good verse would fit here. You likely will be right. Primarily I want you to hear the message I have shared. It is my hope that you will enjoy the book. More importantly is that it will encourage the body of Christ and challenge those who are lost to accept our blessed Savior. Happy reading. Go with God and He will go with you.

Chapter 1
Let's Begin

I don't know of any better place to begin than at the beginning. In this early part of this writing I want to set the stage/the foundation for what is to appear in the chapters that follow.

Have you ever been afraid? I have. Various fears have gripped me for as long as I can remember. Some I have conquered and some may still be clinging to my being. The psychological perspective is that fear is normal, at least to a degree. Oftentimes fear is a survival instinct or reaction. Some apprehensions may just be mild and others far more severe. In the human experience the list of what one may be afraid of is endless. I guess some of the major fears (some of which are familiar to many people) would be such things as being afraid of water, flying, heights, storms, tight places, crowds, doctor/dentist, speaking in front of other folks, and the list goes on. I won't bore you with the fancy and official names of these dreaded culprits. I have heard it said that there are four "primal" dreads: darkness, being alone, heights, and death.

My fears? Well, if I review my whole eighty years on this earth, the list is somewhat lengthy. As a small child, I had fits with the dark, water, being alone, storms, and anything related to death and dying. I was even afraid of carnival rides, as well as fireworks. As I got older the darkness bothered me less and less. I overcame the water bit when I learned to swim at age 12. Now, that doesn't mean I am suggesting that we don't maintain a healthy respect of water sports. It is common sense to proceed with caution. What about being alone? As a youngster I found security in my mom and dad and my older sister. Of course, in the natural course of things, as I grew older my comfort zone improved. My mom, dad, and sister were all uneasy during storms. Joanne (my sister) was terrified of storms (at least during my growing up years). Storms? When I was in third grade, my sister who was eight and a half years older than I was, were at home alone while our parents were working third shift. During a storm one night lightning hit our house and did significant damage inside and outside the house. A ball of fire shot through the rooms of the house. That was quite traumatic for both of us. Joanne also didn't do well with animals, everything from our parakeet Pretty Boy when he escaped his cage, to a number of others among the various species. She saw them all as predators. Flying? My parents were of the mindset that a million dollars would not be sufficient for them to agree to fly in a plane. That terror was handed down to me. Little did I know that as a grownup I would take to the airwaves many times in the states and to other countries. Fireworks? For years now I have thoroughly enjoyed them. The last one I will elaborate on is the death and dying impact. I think that trepidation came from my mom. All her life she struggled with anything about death. I am confident that it was a result from her childhood. She had an older sister and older brother who died when she was a young girl. Lulu was 16 and Lewis was 25. The "undertakers" came to mom's home and embalmed the bodies in the home on the two separate occasions. They proceeded to empty the blood in the outhouse, that she had to use daily. Afterwards, the bodies were "laid out" in the living room. Mom had a visual of that from her bedroom. That was a lot of trauma for a little girl. It is interesting that I eventually transitioned to being a minister at the bedside of dying parishioners, conducting numerous funerals, and working for three funeral homes. Back then we also provided ambulance services. My first introduction to the preparation room (prep or embalming room) was by a mortician friend I met when I was a college student. I spent time with him and his staff regularly. The first embalming I watched was done on a male whose body had been autopsied. Quite an educational, though graphic, experience. During the thirteen years I spent with the sheriff's department, I saw and helped work more than my share of fatal accidents, suicides, and homicides. I vividly recall one incident where I helped the coroner remove a body from a dwelling. The man had been deceased for a few days in the sweltering heat of summer. When I lifted him on my end around the arms and shoulders, his arm exploded on my hand and on my uniform and I was covered with very dark and odiferous blood. The uniform had to be deposited in the trash. It reminds me of how much our first responders should be appreciated and their service respected and honored. Over the years, I have worked closely with (and in some cases had responsibility for) several first responders, including law enforcement, fire and rescue, EMS. On another occasion I assisted at a vehicle accident on the interstate. There was a heavy rain and a tractor trailer and a Chevy S-10 pickup collided. The pickup truck, driven by a lady who was fifty-six with no passengers, was totally crushed. She was killed instantly. She and the truck were shredded. How sad it was to assist the coroner picking up body parts in the median. These are just a couple examples of many. Again, never underestimate the value of those who put themselves on the line to protect others

Why have I talked so much about fear? It is because it is a segway into one of the two main characters who will appear in this writing.

GOLIATH

Who is Goliath?

Physically and biblically he first steps on the stage in 1 Samuel 17:4. You will find his name to be a familiar one. I was first introduced to him as a young lad in Sunday School. One comes to learn quickly that he was a strapping and fearsome fella. His size varies, depending on how you measure it. I Samuel 4 states that he was "six cubits and a span." Mathematically that puts him at between nine and eleven feet tall. Based on cubit and span in the Bible we can safely say he was nine feet or better. Wow! What a big and towering beast. What an intimidator he would be on an NFL line, in the boxing ring, or MMA cage. I practiced and taught martial arts for years. I have earned two blackbelts and I am a certified instructor. If I were chosen (let alone volunteer) for that assignment I would be seeking a substitute to step up to take my place. This guy represented the very epitome of strength and power. I would want at least to have in my hand a .950 Magnum. It is the biggest commercially available sporting rifle cartridge. In Hebrew the name of Goliath as it appears in 1 Samuel usually means giant. This formidable adversary was the "front man" for the Philistine army.

Goliath the mighty warrior was from Gath. According to biblical scholar and author Ryan Nelson, "Goliath was a descendent of the Nephilim–the 'sons of God' and their human wives. The Israelites failed to wipe out the Anakites–a subset of the Nephilim–in their conquest of the Promised Land, and so the Anakites survived in Gath and its surrounding cities, eventually becoming what we know as the Philistines." [1]

---

[1] Ryan Nelson, writer for *OverviewBible*, overviewbible.com, Lakewood, CA., 2022

As if it's not enough for this ferocious warrior to have had so much brawniness, he was loaded down with, covered in protective gear. 1 Samuel 17:5-7 says, "And he had a helmet of brass upon his head, and he was armed with a coat of mail; and the weight of the coat was five thousand shekels of brass. And he had greaves of brass upon his legs, and a target of brass between his shoulders. And the staff of his spear was like a weaver's beam; and his spear's head weighed six hundred shekels of iron: and one bearing a shield went before him." Counting his spear, Goliath was weighted down with around 130 pounds or more of gear. Personally, I would not even be able to struggle out to the battlefield with that much gear, let alone be able to fight. Oh, when I was a young man and strong, I could toss bales of hay around for hours upon hours. Those days are now gone. Relying here on the KJV Old English wording leaves us a little bewildered…in terms of understanding what he was wearing. Perhaps a little breakdown will help. The helmet was some type of bronze headgear, probably an Assyrian type; coat of mail to cover his torso with some kind of scales likely attached to either a leather or fabric backing (which would make it flexible); greaves made for covering the shins and lower legs; target of brass or bronze would have been a breastplate. The common practice for a soldier was to be protected head to toe, as much as possible. His spear "was like a weaver's beam", meaning a heavy duty wood pole such as a loom would contain for processing fabric. In other words, he carried a big "stick" and did not "walk softly."

Spiritually, Goliath in this book is a representation, manifestation of all that is evil and wicked. I am using the term as a representation of the evil one...Satan, Lucifer, serpent, tempter, Beelzebub, dragon, father of lies, prince of darkness, accuser, attacker, etc. We face his attacks daily. This enemy is on the job, so to speak, twenty-four hours a day, seven days a week. The havoc wreaked and subversion of this enemy is deliberate and relentless. Why? Losing his position in Heaven and being cast out of that realm left him bitter, vengeful, vindictive, and a hater of God. The rebellion fostered by him and other angels who unwisely followed his lead caused him to lose his situation. Yes, he will continue down that path until the one thousand millennial reign for binding, and later to be cast into the lake of fire permanently......forever for eternity. In the next chapter I will discuss the enemy's greatest competition and competitor. Can Goliath, this macabre individual, really be dispatched on the battlefield and in our lives?

Chapter 2
Next on the Stage

So far, I have referred to characters stepping on the stage. I certainly lay no claim to the theater. My theatrical experience at best is limited. My first appearance on a stage (more notably platform) was when I was a small boy. At that time my parents, sister, and I were attending the Ridgeway Church of the Nazarene in Ridgeway, Michigan. I was asked to participate in an Easter play. I was only assigned maybe 5 or 6 lines. The director of the play referred to it as a "piece." Well, I memorized the lines. Performance on Sunday morning came. My turn came. I assumed my position on the platform and began to recite my lines. By about line 2 or 3, I froze. The lady who was on the front pew as a prompter kept giving me word by word. I decided it was a lost cause and ran off the platform in tears. I believe that was my earliest decision that public speaking was not in my future. Other than being required to stand in front of the class to recite various assignments in elementary school, junior high, and high school – I don't recall another time I was asked to stand in front of a bunch of people (at least that experience did not happen for a long time). My next prompting to do so was during my senior year of high school. The high school band/chorus director was once again preparing for the annual band follies show. Tryouts were underway. The role of the Master of Ceremonies was up for grabs. Six junior young men were scheduled to audition for that spot. Some of the young ladies in my class wanted me to audition for it. Of course, I quickly declined. They had heard me sing along with pop music bands while dancing with them at high school dances. Big time "romantic Mike." I was just trying to be cool and charm the gals. For some reason they decided I could sing. They were far more confident than I was. Anyway, under duress I folded and said yes to the audition. My classmates wanted a senior to slide into the Master of Ceremonies slot. Time came for the auditions. I was very nervous and so terribly anxious. I stood at the piano where the band director, Richard Wagner, was seated and ready to play. He points to a piece of sheet music and asks, "Do you know this song?" The song? Moody River. I told him I had heard of it. He sang a few bars and then asked me to follow suit. I did. Not much was said. I returned to the classroom. A few days later he called me back to his office to tell me that of the 7 of us, I was selected. Wow! I would not have wanted to hear the other 6. How could I possibly be chosen? So, practices began and were scheduled mornings before classes began and after school. I despised memorization. Yet I was required to memorize my opening solo, monologue that followed, a duet with a freshman girl, a group number, a JFK impression, and the introduction of all the acts of the Broadway type show. We did the performance two nights at our high school for the public, and an afternoon matinee for another high school. It was all overwhelming for me. I had my own dressing room, makeup, tuxedo with changeable jackets of black, white, and red (for different appearances). I played a clarinet in the band during 6th, 7th, and 8th grades. During my 8th grade year, I played with the high school marching and concert bands. That was different. I was able to blend in with the rest of the band members.

Obviously, I still did not envision my going on

to do additional public speaking or other appearances. Little did I know that the future would involve the opposite. With the call to ministry, public office, radio broadcasts, television appearances, substitute public school teaching, etc. –well, you get the picture.

Back to theater, as a young pastor I directed several plays put on by the youth, and portrayed the judge in the play, The Death of a Church. This play was at First Baptist Church, Mt. Vernon, Ky, where I also appeared as a Roman Centurion in an Easter play. Still can't believe I agreed to wear those tights.

As the years went by, I found myself also becoming a Civil War reenactor (training and using my horse as a Union Calvary soldier), as well as later stepping up portraying an 18th century frontier Long Hunter. I suppose one of my more unique roles was that of Santa Claus. I did that for a total of 6 seasons. Among those who may have a more ultra conservative view, this will probably come across as controversial. However, in addition to mall work, parades, private parties, the town Santa, I also was able to reach out to daycares, nursing homes, day treatment facilities, hospitals, and Hospice kids. So many doors opened during those seasons that provided me the opportunity to minister in comforting folks, putting smiles on people's faces, and spreading the good news that Christmas is REALLY all about the birth of Jesus. Some fantasy and stretching one's imagination has been around for a longtime. Nursery rhymes are not real but we tend to bless our children by sharing those with them.

DAVID

Back to the subject at hand, our second character who takes the stage in this writing is someone named David. While I have characterized both Goliath and David as stepping on the stage, in no way am I implying that we are talking about actors or acting. The Bible and even secular history confirms that these two men are very real and the battle between Israel and the Philistine armies is also very real.

David of the Old Testament is a bigger than life character on the earth's stage. He is remembered fondly for so many things. On the other hand, we don't think about him very long until we also recall the heinous sins he committed. That's not so unusual when we think about how easy we find it to see the "bad" in people, rather than the good. There is no denying that David was not perfect and did indeed displease and dishonor the Lord and their relationship. Even so, this shepherd boy through manhood consistently was the person who had a longing to be in relationship and fellowship with and be a servant of God. We are reminded in 1 Samuel 13:14, "...the Lord hath sought him a man after his own heart...." Of course, as one reads a bit further in 1 Samuel, it is learned that David is that man and was anointed by the Prophet Samuel to be King Saul's successor.

As it is not my intention to cover the entire life of David, I do want to mention some of his attributes and even his fall. There is much to be learned from that information. Many books have been written solely devoted to David. It is not my purpose here to try and top those excellent writings which are composed by renown Bible scholars.

This young sheepherder was assigned the responsibility of tending to and guarding the family's sheep. This was crucial for their livelihood. So, while it may have been considered by some to be an unimportant and menial task, it was not that at all. I Samuel 16:12 tells us something of young David's appearance, "....he was ruddy, and withal of a beautiful countenance, and goodly to look to." In simple terms, he was a handsome lad. He had a pronounced complexion highlighted by a red hue.

Perhaps even donned red hair. All of this in that day added to his beauty. He was a rugged but eye-catching dude. Someone who would undeniably stand out in a crowd.

I am familiar with red hair. My paternal grand-mother's maiden name was Chitwood. During my lifetime, it has been rare to meet a Chitwood who did not have red hair. My late wife, Carol, had three sisters. All three had red hair. However, among our children and grandchildren, red hair has surfaced only minimally. During my younger dating years, I dated several girls but only one had red hair. She was 19 and I was 16. Doubt my parents were thrilled with that relationship

We don't know the exact age David was during his sheep caring years and during his other exploits, including when he took out Goliath. Some reputable Bible scholars guess him to be in his late teens or early twenties. This great grandson of Ruth, this handsome musician wrote and probably sang numerous songs, which are reflected in the Book of Psalms. I cannot begin to describe how many of those Psalms have brought comfort to my life over the years, and to millions of others. Thank the Lord for His provision of these songs that speak to our everyday needs.

To say that David plays a key role in God's plans

is an understatement. Earthly speaking, Jesus de-
scended from his linage. His name appears at least
971 times in God's Word. Yes, he is an Old Testament fella. We must not determine that it ends
there. His fingerprints are not absent from the New
Testament. His influence never ends. What do I
mean. Of course, one is how he impacts our lives in
the here and now. Yet, it doesn't end there. Futuris-
tically, it appears that he has a significant place in
eschatology (a fancy term for the Last Days). Here
is where things may get controversial and spur disagreement. There are countless views and interpre-
tations of such a time. I respect those who have
views that differ from mine. My understanding has
developed over the past sixty years or so, my own
reading and study of the Scriptures, and being
taught by and reading after sound and trusted Bible
scholars and theologians. The millennial reign includes three major views. They are premillennialism, postmillennialism, and amillennialism. While
not intending to give exhaustive explanations or
variations of the three views, here is some brief information that goes to the essence of each. Premil-
lennialists believe in a literal earthly thousand years
reign by Christ. Postmillennialists believe that Jesus
comes back after the millennial period. Amillenni-
alists believe that the thousand years is symbolic

and is representative of the church age. I am only touching on the basics.

Early in my ministry I held to the amillennialist view. Why? My home church pastor at that time subscribed to and preached and taught that view. A short time later, during my ministerial studies, I saw much more biblical support for premillennialism. I have embraced that view ever since. Although being somewhat facetious, I have sometimes told folks that I am a promillennalist. Meaning? I'm for however the Lord has decided to do it. Another expression I have heard is "I'm a panmillennialist"…for however it pans out. While these may come across as funny, they don't lack truth. It will be God's way, which obviously is the best way regardless of our understanding, view, and interpretation. Now, back to David relative to the future. What I am getting ready to say coincides with my understanding of last events. The Prophets Jeremiah, Hosea, and Ezekiel all give credence to Jesus being the reigning Messiah and King during the millennium. At the same time, David will serve as His prince. Ezkiel 34:23-24 states, "And I will set up one shepherd over them, even my servant David; he shall feed them, and he shall be their shepherd. And I the Lord will be their God, and my servant David prince among them; I the Lord have spoken it." Whatever you take away from this, do not miss the core message. The Lord is coming back, God is in control, and we need to be ready for His return, both the rapture when we meet Him in the air and enjoy His second coming to the Mount of Olives in Jerusalem, following the Great Tribulation. More about end times in a later chapter.

My battles may be different than some. I am not a military veteran. At age nineteen, I was summoned to appear before my local draft board. This was in the summer of 1965. Upon meeting with them, they learned that I was pre enrolled to begin college in the fall as a ministerial student majoring in religion and was already licensed to preach by my denomination. Still, I returned home with the expectation that I would be drafted. Of course, being the patriot I am, I would have entered the United States Army with no objections. However, shortly after my visit with the draft board, I received a notice that I had been classified by the Selective Service from 1-A to 4-D. The 1-A was for those available for military service, and 4-D designated ministers of religion as exempt from military service. I wanted to serve my country through military service but was also strongly committed to my calling, my license was already in place to minister, and to further my knowledge as a minister through formal training. I was at the ready to hit the ground running to serve in the Lord's army.

Our oldest son, Michael II, joined the Marines. However, he was honorably discharged early due to health issues. He was diagnosed at the Naval Hospital with mitral valve prolapse. While not necessarily life threatening, it can be high risk for the individual who does not get the proper treatment and doesn't take of themself. Michael asked them to let him stay but they refused. Over the years, the U.S. military became very cautious of what may lead to liability and/or disability. Our youngest son, Matthew, joined the Army National Guard. He served for a total of six years.

When I think of military, I often think of battle and fighting. Honestly, in my childhood, adolescence, and high school years I preferred to think of myself as a lover, rather than a fighter. Nonetheless, I had a few altercations and managed to survive them. I was drawn to fighting, as a spectator. My dad loved watching boxing. Television was introduced to the public in 1939, with NBC broadcasting. It wasn't until some years later that we had a television set. I vividly remember sitting by our upright, floor model radio and listening to the Lone Ranger, mom's soap story installments, Amos & Andy, etc. I thought it was great to hear Gene Autry sing Back in the Saddle Again. The first time I recall seeing a television was at some friends' house. A man my dad worked with at the factory had one. We would sometimes go there and watch a boxing match. In fact, the first programming I ever saw on that tiny and snowy screen was boxing.

As a college student I expanded my interest in martial arts by training in judo, taught by Dr. Helvey. Later, I briefly studied Shaolin-Do karate (a Chinese form of kung fu). My instructors were Sensei Elmo Green and Sensei Jim Green. I was tested by the world renown Master Sin The, one of the top practitioners and instructors in the world. Subsequently, I studied Shotokan karate (Okinawan) under the excellent training of Sensei Michael Durham. Mike also holds black belts in various degrees from several styles. Under the tutelage of Sensei Durham for two and a half years, I earned my 1st degree black belt in Shotokan, as well as a 1st degree black belt in a combination style called Aki Ju Kando. For several years, as a certified instructor, I taught self-defense seminars. One of the joys of spending time in martial arts was being able to do it along with our sons, Michael and Matt. Matt was a fellow instructor with me for a few years. In our later years, my late wife, Carol, and I studied Tai Chi for awhile under Master Eric Bullock. Eric has also taught for several years and has much expertise in the arts. Now, as an old guy, for me it is primarily about memories and war stories. I do have good recall of my training, and like the old adage says, "the first mistake is to assume that I'm an old man." Ha! Ha!

Now for a look at the famous battle between the Philistine warrior Goliath and the anointed Israelite David. The battle between the armies of the Israelites and the Philistines is described in great detail in 1 Samuel 17:8-52. Following are some highlights that cover the unfolding of these warring factions:

- Goliath puts himself front and center of the Philistine army. He comes off as a mean, arrogant, overly confident combatant. He taunts the soldiers of King Saul's military force, scaring the daylights out of them, including Saul.

- Goliath proposes a deal. If they kill Goliath, then the Philistine army will become servants to Israel. If the reverse happens, then Israel will be subject to the Philistines. Three older brothers of David were soldiers with Saul. For forty days the giant kept showing up and renewing his challenge.

- Jesse, David's father, sends young David from the sheep to take lunch to his brothers. The battle was fully engaged, and the Israelites were in the trench in the Valley of Elah. While David is there with the food, the big boy Goliath blurts out those same cocky words of challenge. David heard him. David also witnessed the fear of his brothers and their countrymen. In verse 26, David poses a question, "…who is this uncircumcised Philistine, that he should defy the armies of the living God?" His brother reprimanded him and accused who he thought was his "wet nosed" little brother, of neglecting his duties with the sheep and just wanted to see the battle. However, David asks yet another question, as recorded in verse 29, "Is there not a cause?"

- Some of the soldiers heard David and ran and told Saul. In verse 32 David says to Saul. "…Let no man's heart fail because of him; thy servant will go and fight with this Philistine."

- Saul dismisses the whole idea because David is just a kid. How could he possibly be a victor over this trained and hardened warrior? David retorts with his account of shortening the life of a lion and a bear, while caring for the sheep. David quickly informs Saul that the same Lord who enabled him to kill these ferocious animals, will also provide for him as he faces the big, mouthy, and likely smelly Goliath.

- Saul agrees. He further gives this young boy his own armor and sword. David declines, making the point that he has not tested that equipment. He has not been trained in their use. Of course, not to mention that all that garb would be cumbersome – and, probably was thinking, if anything, would interfere with his weapon of choice – namely, a sling.

- David selected five smooth stones from a nearby brook. This stream, or as we Kentuckians would call it "a creek" provided all the ammunition needed. I find it interesting that the ammo came from the Lord. After all, He created both the brook and the stones. David made full preparation with the stones and the sling he carried. In biblical times the sling is not the same as today's modern sling-shot. The sling would have taken extensive practice to build accuracy. Hurling it round and round to gain speed to release the projectile (the stone) explains the mechanics involved required to generate the needed lethal force. It was not a child's toy. It was a for-real weapon. It was a simple weapon yet one that blows my mind relative to gaining expertise with it. Why did David pickup five stones. Only one would be needed to kill Goliath. There are numerous theories and plenty of conjecture out there as to why. The answer? Pretty simple – we really don't know. My own guess would be that the Lord may have not revealed to him that it would only take one stone. Another possibility might be that he took along extra for other enemy combatants. In the mid 1980's, while in Israel, I walked in the Valley of Elah. I picked up five smooth stones in the then dry creek bed and brought them home. I still have them. While in that location, I tried to envision that day, that battle. A very surreal experience.

- After Goliath dismisses David as a ridiculous opponent, David responds with "come on big boy with your big spear and hiding behind a shield" (my paraphrase). He then tells the giant in verse 43, "…but I come to thee in the name of the Lord of hosts, the God of the armies of Israel, whom thou hast defied." In verse 46 he makes it crystal clear to this arch enemy that he is going to kill him, behead him, and leave what is left for wild prey. In verse 47, David states that "the battle is the Lord's." For years, I have used those same words in my daily prayers, to thank the Lord for the truth of those words, and to remind me of my dependence on God to stand in the gap and fight my battles for me. I sure don't want to go any day without knowing He goes before me.

- Under God's anointing and in His power, the shepherd boy does precisely what he said he would do. He kills and beheads the giant. Now, the tables are turned. The Philistine army gets scared and they "get out of Dodge." The Israelites are hot on their trail and knocking them down like bowling pins. I read somewhere that David took 5 stones to the battle and returned with 5. Four were unused and the fifth was in the decapitated head of the giant.

Just as we consider Goliath as a representative, a type of evil, so can we biblically understand David to be a typology of good. Herbert Lockyer explains it this way:

Not only did David prophesy about Christ, he resembled Him in many ways. For example:

Both were born in the humble town of Bethlehem.

Both were of low estate on earth, having no rank to boast of, no wealth to recommend them to the world.

Both were shepherds — the one caring for sheep, the other for souls.

Both were sorely oppressed and persecuted but opened not their mouths.

Both came to kingship. David subdued his foes and had a kingdom stretching from shore to shore. Jesus was born a King, and is to have an everlasting Kingdom. [2]

[2] Herbert Lockyer, *All the Men of the Bible,* copyright by Zondervan Publishing House

You may be wondering how dare I say that David is an antithesis of Goliath. Remember that, while not perfect, not without fault or sin, and even the commitment of some terrible sins (adulterer and murder conspirator) — David is set apart, called by God. He is anointed by the prophet called Samuel. Also remember that if the Lord waited to call those who are "holy," well He would wait for longer than we can count. We know that David was lacking in different ways and was not a sinless creature but never stopped loving God. He served our Heavenly Father time and again. One of the most renown of the Psalms is one of Musician David's 77 that he wrote. Which one? Psalm 51. After the "cardinal" sins committed, David is faced with the Prophet Nathan's rebuke.

The fifty first Psalm reveals the King's remorse and plea for forgiveness. This isn't just some daily routine of asking for forgiveness, followed by bless this food we are about to eat. This is a passionate grabbing the "horns of the altar" praying. This former sheepherder not only admits his guilt and begs for forgiveness but cries out for restoration. This standard of earnest praying continues to be used by millions. You might say, "well, I don't need to go that far in praying. After all, I have never committed adultery or murder." Are we sure? James 2:10,

"For whosoever shall keep the whole law and yet offend in one point he is guilty of all." It goes to the matter of who will cast the first stone. Honestly, do we dare worry about the splinter in the eye of others, and then ignore the big board floating around in our own eye? Yep, that's Scriptural! No wonder Jesus taught, as recorded in Matthew 7:1-2, "Judge not, that ye be not judged. For with what judgment ye judge, ye shall be judged."

Now folks, that's pretty serious stuff. Peter in in 1 Peter 2:21 admonished his readers, "follow his steps" (Jesus). Boy that is a safe way to go. Unlike the devil who tries his hardest to lead us down the wrong road—the path of Jesus leads us exactly in the direction we all need to travel. I cannot begin to tell you how not following the right trail at different times in my own life has culminated in regret and consequences, the natural result of my actions. David was forgiven and restored. You and I can have that same experience when we have sinned. However, we must not ignore what the natural consequences of our actions and sins may be.

Yes, David got it. Even though he became the one who succeeded Saul as king, after both Saul and Jonathan were killed in battle, he still faced those natural repercussions of his earlier sins. He had several wives and children, including his son Solomon who would succeed him, and all of that didn't exactly go smoothly. Yes, he got it. What did he get? It is like the old saying, "Do the crime, do the time!"

Examples of the king's punishment are some things that happened in both his personal and political life. Nathan firmly and pointedly made it clear that the painful assault would never leave his home. Events such as he and Bathsheba, with whom he had the affair, losing the child that was born from that relationship. It didn't help matters that his son, Absalom, turned against him and broke his heart. I suspect it wasn't exactly easy for the king when David's daughter, Tamar, experienced rape by Ammon, David's son. Ammon was born to the household of David by another wife. So, Ammon was a half brother to Tamar. I have to tell you, the family dynamics in that house left a lot to be" desired. A long way off from the sitcom from several years ago, "Ozzie & Harriett."

As I reflect on my own past, particularly my growing up years, I quickly realize that my parents were not perfect, my sister wasn't perfect, and I certainly have never been even close to such a state. I will be rather transparent in the chapters that follow about my journey—the good, the bad, the ugly. Why? I am committed to be honest and up front for the purpose of even helping one person in their journey, and hopefully more. God truly does bring beauty from ashes.

Chapter 3
Goliath Needs Dispatching from Our Early Years

The year was 1945. President Franklin D. Roosevelt died of a brain hemorrhage and Vice-President Harry S. Truman was sworn in and assumed the role of the 33rd President of the United States. It was the year Bess Myerson was chosen as Miss America. The first atomic bomb was detonated at Alamogordo, New Mexico, Hitler committed suicide, and Mussolini was executed. A much lesser event was the birth of a baby that year.

It was Friday, October 5, 1945. In the delivery room of the Maple Knoll Hospital in Cincinnati, Ohio (Glendale), the clock ticked 4:45 pm. The first cry of life reverberated throughout the room. The 29 year old mother had just given birth to her baby.

The male child's parents were Lonnie Bryant and Delphia Vaughn Bryant. Delphia's sister, Irene, got them to agree on the name—Michael Wayne. Yep, yours truly. This was the fourth child to be born to this Bryant family.

My DNA reveals that I come from an ancestry of the following:

- England & Northwestern Europe 36%
- Ireland 27%
- Scotland 20%
- Sweden & Denmark 5%
- Wales 5%
- Norway 4%
- Germanic Europe 2%

My paternal great grandparents were Bausley and Mary Bryant from Wayne County, Kentucky. My great grandfather, on my grandmother's side of the family, was J. R. Chitwood, born in Winfield, Tennessee. In summary, my paternal grandparents were Joe Edward Bryant and Ida Mae Chitwood Bryant, born in Monticello, Kentucky (Wayne County) and Winfield, Tennessee (Scott County) respectively. My dad, Lonnie Bryant, was born at home in Coolidge, Kentucky (Whitley County).

Through redistricting, it later became Whitley City (McCreary County). My dad would often joke about his birthplace being non-existent. Dad was born on September 25, 1911.

My mom was born at home in Elihu, Kentucky (Pulaski County) on May 14, 1916. Her parents were Marion Richard Vaughn and Rosa Angeline Daulton. My Grandpaw Vaughn was born in Glasgow, Kentucky (Barren County). My Grandmaw Daulton Vaughn was born in Naomi, Kentucky (Pulaski County). Naomi is a community within Nancy, Kentucky.

At this point, I think it might be helpful for the reader to understand why I am talking about my background and my family. There are two reasons. One, is to eventually weave this into an illustration that will lend itself to a better understanding of how Goliath assaults our heritage, our past, our growing up years. Secondly, is that I am intentionally inserting biographical bits and pieces in this writing to leave behind for my kids, grandkids, and great grandkids. Some years ago, I constructed a far more detailed biography for them to have when I am no longer around. We are all, as God's creative genius, a composition of mind, soul, and body. No one is immune from Satan's sly, deceptive, and voracious attacks. He desires to devour us.

When dad was 21 and mom was 16, they got married on March 4, 1933. Of course, this was during the time period 1929-1941, known as The Great Depression. Dad had grown up with 5 brothers and 1 sister. Mom grew up with 4 brothers and 6 sisters. Mom and Dad lived in Pulaski County for awhile after they were married. During that time, two sons were born to them. James Edwin was born on November 17, 1933, and died of pneumonia just 3 months later, February 19, 1934. Rodney was born and died on July 19, 1935. I cannot imagine losing one's first two children. Later, my sister, Joanne, was born on January 27, 1937. I look forward to joining my family in Heaven and meeting my two brothers for the first time.

Sometime in 1935 my parents migrated north (along with countless others during those depression years). They spent 11 years in Cincinnati, Ohio trying to eke out a living. After my sister was born, it was about 8 years and 8 months before I was born. When I was around 4 months old, my parents, my sister, and I boarded a bus for Michigan. While in Cincinnati dad worked in various jobs. I recall one was a sheet metal industry, and he was firing coal on the B & O Railroad steam locomotive at the time I was born. The move to Michigan entailed finding a job on Pete Campbell's farm in Milan, Michigan.

The latter part of 1946, we moved to my uncle's farm (mom's brother) on Smith Road in Tecumseh, Michigan. Dad worked there on my uncle's farm for a period of time. Sometime later, Dad went to work at Tecumseh Products Company, where he retired 27 years later. The company made refrigeration units, small engines, and maybe a few other products. When I was three we moved to Holloway, Michigan, where we rented an old farmhouse in the tiny burg. There was a total of a small country school, a general store and post office, a train depot, and a Presbyterian Church. Everything else consisted of farmers and farms. At such a young age, I only have a few memories of those days. However, I do recall some very vividly. We would drive back to Kentucky about every 3 weeks (on weekends) to visit family. Those early post-war years were not particularly prosperous years for us. At the same time, though basically blue collar, somewhat "poor" folks, my dad always managed to provide sufficient shelter, and we did not go hungry. Looking back, I think the simplicity of those days for some reason comforts me till this day. Playing cowboys in my bibbed overalls, riding a homemade stick horse, the garden out back, the brownish/yellowish pull-down window shades, the galvanized round tub for baths, even the outhouse. Also, who said we didn't have indoor plumbing? After all, at night, we had the chamber pot and a coffee can. Yep, that was some real technology there. Hearing the voice of John Cameron Swayze giving the six o'clock evening news (actual news, not everyone's opinion, like today). There was the smell of mothballs but mostly was overcome by the aroma of Mom's cooking. The railroad for the Wabash trains ran right next to our house. How I loved waving to the engineer and him waving back. My first time to recall a "spiritual" memory was the Presbyterian Church ringing its church bells on Sunday mornings. Although we did not attend church much at that time, there is something about that memory that touches me till this day. We never attended that church.

When I was four, that old farmhouse burned to the ground on a Sunday morning. We barely escaped. We got a few photos and lost almost everything else. The Church of the Nazarene in Ridgeway, Michigan, which was about eight and a half miles from where we had been living in Holloway, came to our rescue. Mom and Dad were so impressed with the church's magnanimous gesture that we accepted their encouragement to attend church there on a regular basis. We had attended a few times before the house burned. The generosity displayed far exceeded anything we would have expected, especially from a church that was no larger than that one. I will talk more about my spiritual journey in a later chapter.

Of course, out of necessity, we moved again. This time was to an apartment in Blissfield, Michigan. We only spent a year in that town. Then, we moved to a rental house in Britton, Michigan when I was five. I completed kindergarten there. We moved again from that rented house to a house that Dad was building for us in Tecumseh. It wasn't finished when we moved in. With minimal help, Dad built the house himself. It was located on property we purchased from Mom's brother. I finished growing up in that house. There were two of Mom's brothers who lived next door in front of us. It was so cool to live near some of my cousins.

When we moved to the house on Kaiser Road in Tecumseh Township, we were in the Clinton school district. We were a mile and a half from Tecumseh and 3 miles from Clinton. It is just the way the school district lines were drawn. So, I started first grade at Clinton and graduated from there. Clinton is a small Village and the school had a small population. There were only 47 of us in my high school graduating class. I loved it there and we were a close-knit student body. I cannot imagine going to elementary, junior high, or high school anywhere else. Even though hundreds of miles from Clinton now, I still stay in contact with several of my fellow graduates on social media. Sadly, many have now left us. Keep in mind that I graduated from high school over 62 years ago.

Growing up, I loved the fall season more than any of the other three. I still do. It was the month of my birthday, football season, cool and crisp air, the transitioning of the leaves from summer's green to the brightly colored orange, red, and yellow. Also, it was the opening of pheasant season. That was a special time of year because we would have family from Kentucky and Ohio who would join us to hunt the fields. October was my favorite. I really didn't mind winter. Yes, being in a flatland in the north, there was plenty of chilling wind and unbelievable snow drifts. As a kid, I was mostly oblivious to all of that. For me, it meant ice skating, sledding, building snow forts, snowball fights, and making snow angels on the ground. I felt the frigid weather, and it was uncomfortable. During that time, we didn't have today's technology to keep warm. Nonetheless, hot chocolate, sweaters, wool outerwear, and at least some long handled cotton underwear took up the slack.

During the summers, beginning at age 14, I

worked on farms, and also for an excavator. Long hours, hot conditions, and hard work but I slept well in those days.

Academically, I was an average student in elementary school, got terrible grades in seventh and eight grades, and finally got my head on straight by my freshman year of high school. Grades were good and I was inducted as a member of the National Honor Society.

Now it seems humorous to me when I think about Saturday trips to the corner 5 & 10 cent store. Mom would give me a dime when I was little. There were so many items on the shelves for ten cents that I needed to peruse the merchandise for a long time before making my purchase. I grew up in farm country. Between my parents instilling a strong work ethic in me and constantly being around hard-working folks (especially those who worked the farms and/or worked in industry), I understood early on the importance of managing resources and not wasting money.

Growing up, what did we do as a family. We attended church, hunted, fished, camped, went to auctions, took Sunday afternoon drives, visited family and friends, played monopoly, played Rook and croquet. Night activity was basically watching one of our three channels on television. Honestly, while not perfect, I would not trade the way I grew up. Another bonus for me was knowing and conversing with three grandparents (my maternal grandmother died before I was born), three great aunts, and three great uncles, all born in the 1800's. While I was growing up most of our vacations were spent in Kentucky. Listening and learning from those family members from the 19th century have stayed with me until this day.

Finally, I will stop boring you with my mundane life while growing up.

The point of this chapter? Goliath, the enemy, (Satan) begins his attacks on us from the time we take our first breath. In his relentless efforts he perpetuates the assaults until we take our last breath. The Scripture is quite revealing about this matter.

The poet David said in Psalm 51:5, "Behold, I was shapen in iniquity; and in sin did my mother conceive me." There is no doubt in my mind that infants and young children are automatically covered by the blood of Jesus, certainly up to the age of understanding Christ's death on the cross and their need of a savior. However, the "original sin," borne out of the Garden of Eden's transgressions by couple Adam and Eve have contaminated every human being born since. We don't grow into salvation, it's a choice. We don't grow into sin. It is there at the beginning. What happened in the Garden wasn't God's plan or intention. In fact, the opposite of that is what's real. The Lord, while not required, freely continued creating human life (though contaminated) yet with that same free moral choice. He had the ability to make us robotic but wanted a living, breathing human being with a choice to love Him back. Love him back? What does that mean? Romans 5:8, "…God commendeth his love toward us, in that, while we were yet sinners, Christ died for us." No, we don't in any way, shape, or fashion merit or deserve such a demonstration of God's love but He made the first move. We need to understand that move. It reminds me of our first grandson, Hunter Stewart. When he was a little fella, I would sit down on the floor with him and engage in a game of checkers. Of course, at the beginning it was necessary to teach him how to play. He was so young at that time and it was quite a challenge. Our first game went like this: Me: "Hunter, it's your move." He sat there. I repeated the need for him to make a move. So, taking me at my instruction, he moved his body back a few inches from the game board. We had to work after that on clarifying what "move" meant. We need to be crystal clear that God, not us, made the first move. The Bible states in 1 John 4:19, "We love him, because he first loved us." God desires our fellowship. 1 John 1:3, John says, as he writes to Christians, "…truly our fellowship is with the Father, and with his Son Jesus Christ."

Genesis 1:26 states, "And God said, Let us make man in our image, after our likeness…" Another quick example (among many others) is found in Joshua 24:15, "…choose you this day whom ye will serve…" Early in our lives we start making choices, making decisions. Those become increasingly more as we age. At some point we assume the responsibility of employing discernment and hopefully good judgment and eventually wisdom. Of course, Goliath wants us to not use discernment but to be confused. Our youngest son, Matt, brought his second grade report card home. I commended him for getting all A's but did not understand why he got a B in conduct. His reply? "I don't know, I don't even know when it starts." Seeing conduct as a subject, I guess he thought he was doing well without ever doing anything in that class.

Indeed, we fight Goliath from the cradle to the grave. Make no mistake. Never underestimate the enemy's cunning, deception, subtleness, and his pure evil intentions. He is on the job 24/7. No breaks, no sleep. That monster digs his heels in and foaming at the mouth he will accomplish his mission: steal, kill, and destroy! (John 10:10). Sure, he doesn't approach us in a red suit with pointed ears and a pitchfork. He is far more subtle than that. In fact, the Bible says he appears as an angel of light (2 Corinthians 11:14).

No matter our growing up years, or the remaining years of our presence on earth, we always have a choice. Seems the only wise decision, the only common sense action is to accept what John also describes in John 10:10, "...I am come that they may have life, and that they might have it more abundantly." God is a supernatural being with supernatural powers. He doesn't just do "things," He possesses the ability to do the impossible. That's what Jesus said, and I always take Him at His Word. In Matthew 19:26, "...with God all things are possible." Do you believe the Bible, the holy, perfect, inerrant, infallible Word of God? I do. I sure hope you do. It says in Numbers 23:19, "God is not a man that he should lie..." Move onto the New Testament in Hebrews 6:18 which clearly says that it is "...impossible for God to lie..." Contrast that with the wicked characteristic (or should I say character flaw) of our Goliath, the giant, the evil one. Jesus emphatically declares in John 8:44 about Satan "...there is no truth in him..." and "...he is a liar, and the father of it."

Chapter 4
Goliath Must Be Dispatched from **All** Past Mistakes, Failures, Sins

Here is something profound — we all have a past, a present, and a future. Well, perhaps not so profound but there is a point to be made here. It seems I have wished for redo's or do overs a million times during my 80 years, as a temporary resident on this earth. Of course, wishing doesn't make that possible. No magic wand and no magic bullet in our life's arsenal. Praise the Lord for the depth of His love, for His amazing grace, His marvelous mercy and patience, His incredible forgiveness.

What about you? Do you struggle with the Lord's willingness to forgive you? Oh, I have numerous times. It's not through any disbelief that He can and will forgive me. The Bible is replete with His promise of forgiveness. I'll just share some of those promises the writers of the Word meticulously recorded under the divine and inspired leadership of our Lord. The great news is that when we receive Jesus as our Lord and Savior, He forgives our past, present, and future sin. The pivotal point at which he accomplished that is His death on the cross. He died for every person who has ever been born or will ever be born. He did not shoulder some of our sins but ALL of them. The key for us is unreservedly and personally accepting what He did on that old, rugged cross. He took the sin, the curse, the eternal death, the doom and replaced all of it with eternal life for believers.

I don't feel worthy of God's love, Jesus' death, or the promise of eternity with Him. I certainly never felt worthy of being called to the ministry. I did not view myself as a good candidate for such a call. I still don't feel worthy and never will — but I am eternally grateful and humbled.

Forgiveness is not something we wish were available. It is available. It's not a fable but it's as real as it gets. I stand (so to speak) on God's Word. In fact, I have staked both my life and death on its truth. Now, here are just a few examples of His promise of forgiveness.

The psalmist says in Psalm 103:12, "As far as the east is from the west, so far hath he removed our transgressions from us." Daniel weighs in on chapter 9:9, "To the Lord our God belong mercies and forgiveness, though we have rebelled against him." Jesus said in Matthew 6:14, "For if ye forgive men their trespasses, your heavenly Father will also forgive you." In Colossians1:14 the Apostle Paul writes to the believers at Colosse, "In whom we have redemption through his blood, even the forgiveness of sins." Hebrews 10:17 the author of the book points out this, "And their sins and iniquities are no more." The Lord deliberately made our access to this wonderful forgiveness very simple. Listen again to the words in 1 John 1:9, "If we confess our sins, he is faithful and just to forgive us our sins, and to cleanse us from all unrighteousness." This verse doesn't say that because God is love that everyone automatically receives forgiveness. It says "IF." The English poet, Rudyard Kipling, in his most famous poem called IF, framed it this way in a partial line, "If you can keep your head…" If we can keep our head, our mind that causes us to confess our sins, then we have done it all.

While the Bible is packed with forgiveness verses, I have just shared a few to launch us into my relative thoughts about dispatching Goliath from our past. I know of many people who have struggled with their past. Plenty of examples in the Scriptures. A few who make that list are Paul (formerly known as Saul), King David, Moses, Samson, even Joseph's brothers who sold him into slavery. These are just a few of many on the list.

When it comes to the past and needing forgiveness, I see myself as Exhibit A. I have messed up, failed, made poor decisions, used faulty discernment, have been disobedient, missed the mark, committed sins of omission and commission. I have found it necessary on numerous occasions to repent. Penance is nothing new to me. I have found myself thinking that was crazy, that was foolish, how could I be so dumb? I strongly suspect that many of you reading this book may be able to relate to my experience with the past. I messed up at times in my childhood, my adolescent years, my teens, my young adult life, my middle age, and my senior years. I am certainly not proud of any of it. Frank Sinatra and Elvis Presley popularized the song "My Way." In recounting his life, the singer says he has had only a few regrets. I wish I could say that. To be completely transparent, I think my regrets would more rightly belong in the category of "many."

One of the biggest and most sorrowful regrets I have, occurred in the year of 1964. Four months after graduating high school, I turned 18. About a month after that, I met a young girl at a church my family and I began attending. She was only 14. I know, too young. Anyway, after awhile, with her parents' permission, we began dating. While I was still 18, she turned 15. We dated for 8 months. Though both of us were young, our relationship became very close and we fell in love. After dating for three months or so, I really began experiencing the call to ministry. That caught me completely by surprise. We were both active in church. I was not interested in ministry as part of my life's plans. Yet, I knew the divine call was real. I didn't want to surrender to that call. I will admit that I was miserable in my struggle with the matter. I wanted to do what God wanted me to do but just could not see it as a fit for me. First and foremost, I felt extremely unworthy of that call. The girlfriend and I continued to date. I shared with her the call I felt. She was supportive. I can't say her parents were not supportive but if they were it was quiet. I guess many parents dislike the idea of a daughter eventually marrying a preacher, who most likely will not make a lucrative living.

The pastor even had me speak a couple of times. I wanted to be obedient but it was like trying to get a jumbo jet off the ground. After we had dated for those 8 months, things began to go south between my girlfriend's parents and me. They were good people. Up to that time, I had a close relationship with them. I think the more serious the relationship became the more concerned they became. Years later, after raising two daughters of my own, I was much better at understanding where the parents were coming from. The only disclaimer I am offering is them telling her she was no longer allowed to date me, after as long as we had been a couple. That's a tough assignment for two young people who have been dating for 8 months. It just wouldn't work. We were too in love and quietly rebelled. To make a long story short, we did something that was not wise. We ran away, with the plan to get married. We soon learned that laws had changed in states that were once very liberal in allowing underage couples to marry without parental permission. Obviously, after disappearing and ending up in another state far away from our home (Winston-Salem, NC) where I worked for three months, things didn't end well. We returned home voluntarily but under some duress (we were never located by the authorities) I was arrested, pleaded guilty, and ordered by the court to never be near my girlfriend or her family ever again. Of course, my heart was broken and so was hers. Our feelings for one another had not changed. I was charged with contributing to the delinquency of a minor. Even though I was still a teenager myself, I was legally an adult. I was fined, and given sixty days in jail. This was a long way from my call to the ministry. It's an understatement to say I had plenty of time to mourn, reflect, pray, and seek God's forgiveness while incarcerated.

I was housed in a cell that had 3 block walls, and one section of bars. That cell was setup in a barracks style. There were 12 steel bunks (that mostly stayed full), a steel table and benches, 1 shower stall without a curtain, 3 commodes without seats. The shower and toilets were in plain view of all the other inmates. All the comforts of home – NOT. I was issued 1 pair of coveralls a week, and 3 meals a day (I would not hire that chef). Everything was nailed down and all dishes and cups were metal, with a tablespoon for eating. I was allowed only one fifteen minute visit a week through a speaker and a tiny scratched up glass (which hardly allowed me to see my parents on the other side). I was housed with prisoners of all types. Some were in for misdemeanors, some for felonies. Some were hardened felons on their way back to state prison. Yeah boy, I was hanging with some great folks. These would normally not be the individuals one would choose for their social circle. However, the way I saw it, I was no better than any of them. After all, I'm incarcerated with them. I was feeling hopeless. I was heartbroken at the loss of my girlfriend, I was ashamed, I was embarrassed, and I knew I had blown the divine call. I can't deny, even with the Lord forgiving and forgetting my sin, to no longer hold it against me — to this day it is still a sword that will never depart, just as it was with King David. I call it again, the natural consequences of my actions.

Well, with 10 days credited for good behavior, I pulled 50 days in the big house. I was only out of that cell twice during the 50 days. Once, for a brief court appearance and once for about 15 minutes to mop a hallway. Yes, it will always be etched in my memory of perhaps the longest 50 days in my life. Long days and long nights under my scratchy, wool blanket. No air conditioning during the early hot days and very little warmth when the temperatures plummeted. Some high up windows were cracked open. From a top bunk I could look out and see a little of the treetops. Leaves were green at first, then changed colors, and then were on the ground when I was released. I spent my 19th birthday inside those bars. It certainly was not the preferred way to spend my favorite season of the year.

I returned home with my parents. Thankfully, though not happy with what had transpired, they were welcoming and helpful. I spent some time in the valley of despair and depression. Sort of felt like my life was over. Guess I had a bit of the Elijah experience when he sat under the Juniper tree and wanted to give up. The company where I had been working as a machine operator when I left for "parts unknown", graciously gave me back my job. At least, I was a good worker when I was with them before. I did have to start at the bottom again. It was okay. I felt blessed to have my job back. I worked there for about another eight or nine months, before moving to Kentucky to attend college.

The day I was released from jail was on a Sunday morning. Mom prepared a great breakfast when we got home. That night we attended church. At this time my mom and dad were back at my home church. It was good to go back there. Of course, I felt very conspicuous because of what I just had experienced. Even so, during that Sunday night service at church I went forward when the pastor gave the invitation. I had never met him. He tried to visit me while I was in jail but the officials denied it. That night I was very broken, very guilty, very penitent. I wept. I made an "acknowledgment" in front of the congregation that night. That was somewhat traditional among Southern Baptist churches at that time. The pastor and congregation, with what seemed to be a forgiving spirit, were so loving and caring. Even though I knew I would never be in the ministry, I was thankful to be getting my life back on the right path and to be in a good relationship with the Lord once again.

Over the next little while, the pastor and I became good friends. He had moved from Middlesboro, Kentucky to accept the pastorate in Tecumseh, Michigan at the Tecumseh Missionary Baptist Church—my home church. I shared with Pastor Seal Janeway how sorry I was that the possibility of my becoming a minister was now null and void. He disagreed with me, reminding me of how many folks the Lord used in the Bible who had messed up. He encouraged me to rethink and pray about the matter. Reluctantly, I did. The lord again began working in my life, reminding me of His call on my life. The pastor asked me to walk beside him in his ministry. I did that for the next 9 months. He became my mentor. He told me about Cumberland College in Williamsburg, Kentucky (later to become the University of the Cumberlands). After those several months of accompanying him during ministerial activities, I enrolled by faith at Cumberland. I had the required academic standing but no funds.

No one in my immediate family had gone to college. I actually didn't think I was smart enough to do it. I was short on confidence, not just money. My mom quit school in her junior year to marry dad. She was a straight A student. Dad didn't even complete sixth grade. My sister graduated from high school. I also continued in faith for the next four years of higher learning. I earned my way by sweeping the dorms and later working in the President's office and public relations. I was a ministerial student majoring in Religion and minoring in Sociology. Little did I know I would later earn a master's and doctorate—or see my kids and grandkids attend and graduate from the same institution. Between the kids, grandkids, and spouses—along with attendance and graduation at several other universities, they made their mom and me very proud of them. I did not know what seed I was planting at what later became my alma mater. (In addition to myself, six of our family members later earned bachelors, four masters, and 4 others completed part of their undergraduate work there). Quite soon I was getting invitations to speak at some of the religious organizations on campus, as well as being invited to preach at some of the local churches.

The girlfriend I had lost in 1964 was not my first

or last love. She was everything to me when we were dating. When I was 12 years of age, I liked a 12 year old girl, who happened to be the pastor's daughter in that church. First girl I ever kissed. I admit, too young. Between being released from jail and going off to college I did date a little but nothing serious. I dated several girls when I was in high school. I "went steady" once when I was fifteen. However, I enjoyed "playing the field" (as Barney Fife might say) during my high school years. Dated some pretty cool girls, including four cheerleaders. Not long after going to college I met and dated a sweet, Christian girl there in Williamsburg, Kentucky. Loved her family. I liked her a lot but didn't love her. I eventually broke up with her. Now the tables were turned. She would have married me. I broke her heart. I felt so terrible. I knew what it was like to be on that end of the relationship. My soulmate was still out there somewhere. More about that in a later chapter.

During my many years in ministry and social work I encountered countless stories of people who were hurting and often devastated. Broken relationships, broken marriages, broken families, those guilty of crimes, etc., etc. I had compassion on them and with God's help tried all I could to help. The years I served as a Christian counselor I found to be challenging yet rewarding. My practice included relationship involvement, marriage, depression, grief, and anger management therapy. I was also receiving court referrals from our local judges.

Bottom line? From the time I was born until the very time of this writing I have been imperfect and flawed. I have a heart for God but the world and the flesh have to be constantly guarded against. Staying in the Word, praying, and trusting the Lord to be able to walk in the Spirit are the difference makers. My Goliath has told me repeatedly that I cannot please the Lord and don't have to worry about pleasing God. Thankfully, only through God's presence and leadership have I been able time and again to dispatch Goliath. So can you! Remember that the enemy is a liar and the father of lies. I want to wrap up this chapter with some encouraging words from the Word:

- Joshua 1:9, "…Be strong and of a good courage; be not afraid, neither be thou dismayed: for the Lord thy God is with thee whithersoever thou goest."
- Isaiah 41:10, "Fear thou not; for I am with thee: be not dismayed; for I am thy God: I will strengthen thee; yea, I will help thee; yea, I will

uphold thee with the righteous hand of my righteousness."

- John 16:33 Jesus said, "...In the world ye shall have tribulation: but be of good cheer; I have overcome the world."
- Romans 8:37, "...we are more than conquerors through him who loved us."
- 2 Corinthians 4:8-9, "We are troubled on every side, yet not distressed; we are perplexed, but not in despair; persecuted, but not forsaken; cast down, but not destroyed."
- Philippians 4:13, "I can do all things through Christ who strengthens me."
- 2 Timothy 1:7 the Apostle writes to young Timothy, "For God hath not given us the spirit of fear; but of power, and of love, and of a sound mind."
- James 1:12, "Blessed is the man that endureth temptation: for when he is tried, he shall receive the crown of life, which the Lord hath promised to them that love him."
- 1 John 4:4, "Ye are of God, little children, and have overcome them: because greater is he that is in you, than he that is in the world'.

Folks, no matter your past, or my past, once we know Jesus the Bible assures us that we have an Advocate, a Mediator. We aren't out in the cold. We are in the care, love and grace of our Lord. We may fail and falter many times in our lives. The Word promises us that He will always be with us. Hebrews 13:5 is a poignant reminder that the Lord says, "I will never leave thee, nor forsake thee." I have depended on this truth more times than I can begin to count. I think in my twilight years more than ever.

In our life's journey, our pilgrimage, we walk through the dirt, the mud, the grime, the crime, the threats, the depression, the valleys, the craziness, the incredible challenges—what is it for you? Sadness, grief, depression, addiction, financial burdens (too many bills and not enough income), storms, hurricanes, cyclones, tornadoes, inherent fears, threat of nuclear war, and the list continues, right? The good news is that we don't have to continue residing in that which disturbs us about our past or frightens us about the present or future. While most of my growing up years were in the house that my dad built at 3886 Kaiser Road, Tecumseh, Michigan, I no longer live there. That's a house from my past. Just as I no longer live in that house, I also no longer need to live and wallow in my past poor choices, mistakes, and sins. They are now "water under the bridge," or as the Bible promises in Micah 7:18-19, "Who is a God like unto thee, that pardoneth iniquity, and passeth by the transgression of the remant of his heritage? He retaineth not his anger forever, because he delighteth in mercy. He will turn again he will have compassion upon us; he will subdue our iniquities; and thou wilt cast all their sins into the depths of the sea." Isn't it wonderful to be covered by His blood?

As my readers, I pray for you to know Jesus and trust in His forgiveness. As one of the hymns of old says, "Trust and obey, for there is no other way to be happy in Jesus, but to trust and obey."[3] Aren't you glad Jesus has dropped all the charges, when we come to Him for cleansing? It happens through justification (which he paid for on the cross). Once we accept Him, we are no longer declared guilty. A simple yet powerful explanation I have heard about justification over the years is "just as if I had never sinned."

---

[3] Trust and Obey," inspired by Dwight L. Moody and written by Daniel Towner and John H. Sammis in 1887

Chapter 5
Dispatching Goliath from Our Marriages

This is a chapter in the book that I approach with mixed feelings. It's an overflow of emotion for me. Not because it is about marriage but because of the personal illustrations. It is not an easy assignment for me, but I am hoping what I share will be encouraging to at least some of my readers.

In 1960, my parents and I began attending the Tecumseh Missionary Baptist Church in Tecumseh, Michigan. The church was located less than two miles from our house. The pastor of the church was Edgar Owens. His wife was Sadie Bolton Owens. Reverend Owens and his family had moved originally, from Tazwell, Tennessee to Jackson, Michigan. Later he would accept the pastorate of the church in Tecumseh. The couple had four daughters. The oldest to the youngest were as follows, Marie, Anne, Mary, and Carol. The three older sisters were quite a bit older than Carol. The first place I know of them living in Michigan was Jackson. Carol was not born until the family moved to Michigan. She was born in Jackson. While Carol was still a little girl, her dad visited Tecumseh and surveyed the town to determine if there were any folks living there who might be interested in starting a Southern Baptist Church in Tecumseh. There was interest. From that seed, he opened the doors in the rented Pithian Hall and they began meeting. The Pithian Hall was a gathering place for members of the Knights of Pythias, a fraternal and charitable organization that was founded in 1864. Later, property was purchased and eventually a church building was erected. The church grew to become a good-sized congregation. It continued meeting there for several years. The building is now owned by a different church. The original organization bought other property and built a new and larger structure.

When we started attending the church in Tecumseh, I was fourteen years old and a freshman in high school. Carol was the same age and a freshman. The first time I remember seeing her was in a Sunday School classroom in the church basement. The class was composed of both teenage girls and boys. There were several sitting around the wall of that room. Although I was of course aware that there were several, it is as though I only saw Carol. I was immediately attracted and taken by her. No, I had no idea about anything in the future but knew I felt this powerful connection to her. I think I dismissed it as she was probably too pretty to be interested in me. Carol was the most beautiful gal I had ever seen. She still is, inside and out. She also came across as quite mature and confident. I didn't know how I could match that. To make a long story short, a little later, she and I became girlfriend/boyfriend. Meeting her was a half moon and becoming her boyfriend was a total eclipse. Obviously, at age fourteen there were significant limitations. I was still bashful. She initiated our getting together. She invited me to a party at her school and invited me to a hayride. Of course, I attended both. We primarily sat together in church and visited back and forth at each other's homes with our parents. I wished we had been in the same schools. When Easter came, I bought her a corsage (an orchid) and dropped it off at her house on the Saturday night before Easter Sunday. Yes, I did inquire ahead of time to ascertain what color dress she would be wearing. Those were special days for both of us.

I am the first to acknowledge the existence of something called infatuation and "puppy love" but it wasn't that for me. I was madly, passionately in love with that girl. Then, the hammer fell. Frankly, looking in retrospect, I think it was one of my encounters with Goliath. He clearly did not want us together. How do I know? Because, despite his attack, time would reveal God orchestrating His plan for this young lady and me.

It was a Sunday morning. We were in Sunday School and then came up for the worship service in the sanctuary. As usual, we were sitting together in church. Sitting in the church pew behind us were three or four boys. Before the service began, they kept talking with Carol, cutting up with her. They were laughing and she was laughing and cutting up with them. It all seemed out of place to me. What was all that flirting about, with me sitting right there with her? Now, Goliath, the green-eyed monster called "jealousy" arrived. When I returned to church that Sunday night I confronted Carol. I explained that I felt embarrassed and uncomfortable. My approach was not very tactful. In fact, it was inappropriately seasoned with a bit of anger. I got "the look" from her. She wasted no time in telling me that we no longer needed to be an item. My heart dropped. I knew I had blown it but was at a loss to know how to regain what I had just lost. I learned the guys were her first cousins visiting from another town. I went home with a broken heart. It was clearly my fault. No one was to blame except me, which added guilt on top of being heartsick. Carol was the most loving person I have ever known but could and would stand her ground when called for.

Time passed. I didn't know how Carol felt. I lacked the courage to ask. I knew my feelings for her had not changed. Young or not, I absolutely loved her and if we had been older (and she would have agreed) I would have married her then. Some months later we each became fifteen. We were cordial but distant. There was no longer an "us." A little more time passed and to add fuel to the fire I learned that she and her family were going to move to Ohio. Her dad had been called as pastor of a church parish in Bellevue, Ohio. Carol would be a long distance from Tecumseh and would finish her last couple of years of high school at Bellevue High School. You got it. Another heartbreak for this ole' boy. At least, as long as she was living in Tecumseh, I thought there was the possibility of us getting back together again. I was depressed. Now it was more than ghosting me, all my hopes and dreams came crashing down. What was I to do? I had no choice but to gather the pieces and go on with my life. The problem was that I could not forget. I could not stop loving her, no matter what. And—I never did!

The song, "Endless Love," written and composed by Lionel Ritchie, is a tribute to the profound, unwavering and eternal devotion of a man who has found the only woman he will ever love.

Carol was my Endless Love!

As most everyone knows, there are different kinds of grief. Death, broken marriages, broken relationships, lost friendships, etc. Even the loss of a job can be devastating. Losing character or reputation is no small thing. Well, I did go on. Carol went on with her life. We dated other people. We finished high school. We sowed some wild oats (I think my sowing was worse). Eventually we found ourselves, after dating different people, in serious relationships with others. They were serious enough to have culminated in marriage but somehow there was still something missing for both of us. A feeling of incompleteness. I am not going to rehash my fall from grace, as I shared with you in the earlier chapter. During the next 5 or 6 years, I only saw Carol on one occasion. Her dad came back to Michigan to conduct a revival meeting at the Clinton Baptist Church, which was located (and still is) in the town where I attended and graduated from public school (years later I conducted a revival meeting at that same church). My mom, dad and I were one of the inaugural families in organizing that church. Carol and her mom accompanied her dad on the trip. Now the two of us were sixteen. I only saw her briefly during the week of the revival but it was amicable. One night after service, a bunch of us teenagers went out to what was supposed to be a haunted house in the country. She told me later that she wanted to be with me that night. There was no doubt that I wanted the same thing. However, guess I didn't read the tea leaves right. Also, I was afraid of yet another heartbreak. Instead, I spent my time with another girl when we were at the haunted house. Oh well, I have never claimed to be that smart and certainly not that intuitive. Better at it now than then. Carol has always possessed the gift of being quite intuitive.

Four more years passed. No contact between us. Both of us graduated from high school. She enrolled in LPN school, dated guys, and worked part time. I only learned about those activities through the grapevine. I went to work in the factory and eventually left Michigan, moved to Kentucky, and enrolled in college. She still dated some. I dated a little during my first semester of college. During the Christmas holidays I went home to my parents in

Michigan. While I was on break, Carol's dad called my parents on New Year's Day, wanting to stop by and see us. They were up from Ohio visiting former church members that had been good friends. There she was again—now the woman, the girl I never stopped loving. Not surprising, it was fireworks all over again for me. Still, I kept my cool. We were both so much more grown up now. I wasn't as bashful and a bit more confident. It was a great visit. I was guarded about getting my hopes up, except that we were both still single. The next morning, I headed back to Kentucky and the campus to get ready for midterm exams.

A few days after returning to campus, I went to the college post office to check my mail. In that mail was an envelope addressed to me from Carol. She was writing on behalf of her dad. He wanted to know if I could possibly be a guest speaker at the Napoleon Baptist Church, Napoleon, Ohio, where he was now pastor. He wanted me to fill the pulpit Sunday morning and evening. There was also an invitation for my parents and me to spend the afternoon at their home. It was a weekend that would work because I would be through with exams and have a short break. I was honored to be invited. Brother Owens had been my pastor. In fact, he baptized my mom, dad, and me. However, being a little wiser and a little more intuitive, I found myself reading between the lines in Carol's letter. Could it be? Was there a hidden message? Was it more than preaching? Did she still have feelings for me? A myriad of questions flooded my mind. I wasn't sure of the answers. No matter. I looked forward to preaching for my former pastor. I decided to remain reticent about thoughts of Carol, even with my parents.

That weekend came. The Owens family lived in Wauseon, Ohio, a short distance from Napoleon. I enjoyed speaking at both services, the first time Carol and her parents had heard me preach. Mom, Dad, and I enjoyed our visit that afternoon. During a conversation with Carol, I found myself (without having planned to do so) asking her if she would be interested in going to a movie in Bowling Green, Ohio the next night. I explained that I would be returning to Kentucky on Tuesday morning. She agreed. Here we go again. The wheels in my head are spinning. The next night I drove back down from Michigan to take her on the date. It was the most unique yet most powerful date I ever experienced. Oh, it started out as a normal date. I cautiously held her hand during the movie. We saw a James Bond film. When I took her back home we sat in the driveway for a little while. We talked and I will just leave it at this—we became "more friendly." Again, with no plan to do so, I asked her if she would be my girlfriend, even though geographically we were a good distance apart. She said yes. I walked her to the door of her house. We were standing in a pitch-black small doorway and could not see one another. Next, I blurted out, "Will you marry me?" Her answer? A resounding YES!!!!! This was in January. We did get to see each other a couple of times between Kentucky and Ohio. We talked on the phone every few days. I called her from a phone booth in downtown Williamsburg, and she accepted the charges for a collect call. Remember, I was a financially poor college student. What I owned, except for my used Ford, you could pretty much put in a suitcase. Years later she would tell folks that she could not be accused of marrying me for my money, because she married a poor college student. Then, I would reply with "But I've been paying for it ever since." *LOL*

We got married in April of that year. The wedding and honeymoon in Niagara Falls took place during my spring break. She had funds from where she had been working to pay for both our rings and the honeymoon. Yes, I finally did make it up to her. Down the road, I finally bought her an engagement ring. It never mattered to her. She was unbelievably low maintenance. Over the years, the kids and I would have to beg her to get things for herself. It was always about what the kids needed, what I needed, or whatever way she could help others. Her folks raised her with a servant's heart.

Carol Owens Bryant was the most selfless, sacrificing, loving, caring, giving, serving, compassionate person I have ever known. She was my wife, my spouse, my best friend, my supporter, my cheerleader. She was truly that "stand by your man" woman. She knew me better than anyone ever had or ever will. She loved me despite my faults. What else? Well, she was the balance, the center, the anchor for our family. Domestically she was a great cook and loved cooking. She was such a talented vocalist and pianist. Her work ethic was unmatched. Whatever she did, she did with commitment and excellence. She was my true soulmate. No man could have ever ordered a better partner, companion, lover. No family could ask for a better mother, mother-in-law, sister-in-law, aunt, or Momo. It was not a thing of labor for her to love God and love people. She demonstrated that daily. In ministry she was both my right and left hands. She sang, she played, she taught, she attended meetings, she was strong and steadfast in the difficult times a pastor often faces. I never had to look around for her. I knew she would be right there. It is often challenging to be a minister's wife. She never wavered, she never gave up. She was a woman of the Word and Prayer. Nothing was too big or too little to pray over. She would lay prayerful hands on the washing machine if it was acting up. She kept up the pace of working at home, several years outside the home, and took care of and raised four kids. In addition to working part time jobs when she was younger, she worked in banking for thirty-one years, worked with tourism, the insurance industry, and as a Main Street Manager for our city. For twelve years (three four-year terms) she once again stepped up to the plate as the City of Mt. Vernon's First Lady. Yep, she was a thick and thin, better or worse, rich or poor lady. I have sometimes said that she earned a Purple Heart for putting up with me. Men aren't always easy. Of course, that can be true of the ladies as well. *LOL*

This unquestionably Proverbs 31 lady changed residences on February 15, 2023, at 4:44 am, less than five hours from the end of Valentine's Day. She walked in dignity and she died with dignity. She passed away peacefully at the Rockcastle Regional Hospital, Mt. Vernon, and her body is interred in the Cresthaven Cemetery next to our church, which is Bible Baptist Church. Our monument only lacks my death date. The front of the marble, arched stone bears the words "Together Forever" and on the back the Scripture "Death is swallowed up in Victory." Inscribed on the back of the monument also are the names of our kids and grandkids. Two weeks before she graduated to Heaven, while in ICU — her first day there, she said to me, "I'm going to Heaven." I replied, "Yes, we are, but not right now. We still have things to do." She said, "You don't understand. It's time. God is very near." She also said, "I see they need another alto in the choir up there." For the last four or five days before she left us, she became unresponsive and then passed in her sleep. The last words she and I exchanged, before she became unresponsive, were "I love you!" I have so much peace about her transition and her destination. In terms of the Last Days, the Lord has a detailed plan that will occur in stages. For example, Rapture, the Great Tribulation, Second Coming, Millennium, Armageddon, final defeat of Goliath (serpent, devil, Lucifer, enemy, etc.) will happen. During the interim it is clear to me from the Bible that our loved ones who die in Jesus are in what we sometimes call the Intermediate Heaven, or Paradise. We can only guess at the particulars but know they are healed, at rest, at peace. "Thanks be to God who gives us the victory..." (1 Cor 15:57

ESV). Does this mean my grief is mild. It does help to know that my sweetheart is in the realm of joy and peace. It does help to know she died peacefully. It does help to know that she is with Jesus. She longed for that day. My grief? Inexplicable! One saying, is, "No love, no grief." However, as bad as it hurts, I would still choose love. I cannot imagine what it would be like to have not loved my soulmate. The grief is deeper than any ocean and bigger than the universe. As I write this chapter, she has now been gone a little over two and a half years. I miss her terribly everyday and every night. I have cried everyday since she was promoted to her real home. Yes, she was promoted, graduated, went into the presence of Almighty God immediately. As an old man of eighty years, I have faced a lot of hard knocks and fought lots of battles during my life. I have the scars and battle worn body and brain to prove it. Praying that I won't outlive my kids or grandkids. I can think of nothing worse than losing my soulmate. We were one. When she left, she took half of me with her. I am so grateful for our kids and their families, and for my friends. The sting of death is real. Is death a punishment? To be escorted into the presence of the Lord by His Holy Angels during the moment of our last breath is a promise fulfilled for the one who knows Jesus. Those of us who are left, although temporarily, feel a gut wrenching sting. Yes, we go on. We do the best we know how to do but things are never the same. Our happiness is not the same. I am grateful that no one can steal the "joy" of the Lord that we have.

As difficult as it was to let my girl go, soon I will be reunited with her and the host of Heaven, and especially Jesus. I truly don't dread death. As the Apostle Paul described, he wanted to stay on earth but longed for Heaven. The process with our bodies that we may go through is another matter. Suffering before leaving this earth is something none of us covet. Carol was relatively healthy until 2007. She had undergone some surgeries and other procedures but was doing well. In 2007 she contracted thyroid and Non-Hodgkin lymphoma cancer. It required major surgery, chemo and radiation. The prognosis early on didn't look promising. With good medical care and the Lord's intervention, she stayed in remission and lived for a little over 15 years. Our son, Michael, told her the Lord had shown him that she would live for another 15 years, and she did. In 2015 she had 6 mini strokes and a major stroke. She began having seizures, but medication did help some with those. In 2017 she had a massive stroke. It required a helicopter ride to Lexington. She could not move even her head on the left side. A blood clot on the right side of her brain the size of Texas had affected the left side of her body. Mentally, she was not herself. Our kids and I were told by the neurologist and the hospitalist that there was nothing they could do for her. The message was fatalistic and not what we wanted to hear. The neurologist told us we would have to pray. I assured him we were and that we had many folks praying. Medical personnel never expected her to survive and leave the hospital alive. We spent 11 days at the hospital, 4 weeks at a rehab facility, and nearly 6 weeks at a nursing home rehab. She was confined to a wheelchair and never walked again. She of course did a prescribed course of therapy for the next 6 years until she left us. She wanted to walk so badly but never lost her spirit, her fight, her attitude, even her sense of humor. Due to the strokes, more medical issues arose but we met all of them head on. We did not forfeit our quality of life. We continued going to church, family events, shopping, eating out, etc. I got her out of the wheelchair and put her in our golf cart and on the back of our ATV with me. I was Mayor during those last six years that she was disabled. It was necessary to hire part time caregivers. That is not an easy task. At least it wasn't for us. We had 12 different ones in 6 years. Greta was our last one. She did an excellent job for us. The others left on their own. No one was fired. We are all still friends. Daughter-in-Law Holly also helped us some with her care. Of course, our kids did all they could.

In summary of paying tribute to my dear wife (and there aren't enough words to fully do justice to that), I want to say that our family and I know the Lord "rescued" her on February 15, 2023. Before she passed, she was diagnosed with congestive heart failure, mild dementia, a threatening UTI, sepsis, double pneumonia, and finally her kidneys and other organs were losing ground. If she could have lived, it would have been very challenging and uncomfortable for her. She would not have wanted that. I would not want that for me. The death certificate lists several causes of death, but we are confident that the sepsis was the ultimate culprit. Although it is not impossible, older people with serious medical issues rarely survive poisoning of the blood stream. We know God took her when it was her time and she knew it better than anyone. I will miss her with my whole being until I am reunited with her.

The Book of Soloman 8:7 (NIV) says, "Many waters cannot quench love; rivers cannot sweep it away..." I have always loved her (since I was 14 years old). I will love her always and forever! She was and is my Endless Love!

Carol and I had discussed the possibility of writing a book together. Sadly, that never came to fruition. We did everything together. When our kids were growing up it was rare for us to get a babysitter. We did almost everything with them. I am so blessed by my family and their support. I don't know why Carol is gone and I am still here. I have certainly had and now have my share of medical issues. I trust God's wisdom. He left me here for a reason. He knows I am open to his will and leadership. In writing this book, I am not alone. First, after much thought and prayer, I am following what I know the Holy Spirit is leading me to do. Second, Carol is on every page. She was a part of me and everything I did. This is OUR book! The words below are copied from an unknown author. They express my feelings so well about Carol.

I'll never stop feeling like
a part of me left with you.
You were my forever, and
even though I lost you,
nothing has replaced you.
My heart still belongs to
you, and it always will.
That's what forever love has become for me -

> endless missing, endless
> loving, without you here.

What about you, my readers? Is your marriage perfect? Is your marriage in trouble? Is it broken? The sad reality is that no marriage is perfect, at least not that I know about. Over the years I have performed wedding ceremonies for countless couples, including all four of our kids and one grandson. As I alluded to earlier, I spent time during my ministry counseling with numerous couples. God has a well-designed plan for marriage in His Word. Its sort of like, "the plan works if you work the plan." Now, I know that's easier said than done. My marriage was by no means perfect. During the 57 years Carol and I were married, we never considered divorce as an option. We, as all couples, experienced the challenges of her being a woman and me being a man. It has nothing to do with the adage "right brain, left brain." In fact, that is a myth popularized by some, that has been debunked. Both sexes use both hemispheres of their brains. However, there are differences in our make up as male and female. Learning to live together in harmony, learning the importance of giving and taking (with an emphasis on giving) is easier for some than others. Many things may play into it. One example would be family background. Carol grew up in a home where everything was taken in stride. The idea was to remain cool, calm, and collected no matter what was happening. My home was very different. Our family was much more reactive to what was going on. The tenor of the two homes was just not the same. Marrying someone calls for lots of adjustments. While not trying to escape the reality of our living on earth in bodies of flesh, at best we are sinners. Some are sinners, and some are sinners saved by grace. And, not to over spiritualize things but I am thoroughly convinced that my marriage to Carol Owens was possible and better because of us knowing and trying to walk with the Lord. Like the song of old, Jesus looked beyond our fault and saw our need. I am glad that we were able to do that. Carol loved me despite my sins, faults, shortcomings, failures. I saw her the same way. I confess that she had the heavy lifting putting up with me in that endeavor. We certainly had times of disagreement. We both had strong opinions. A central matter we always agreed on was that the Lord orchestrated our ending up together and that we both knew we were soulmates. We both said we would do it all over again.

Goliath has no place in marriage. Marriage can be and is supposed to be successful and happy. Our expectations need to become much lower if we refuse to know the Lord and serve Him. A marriage partner should be cherished and put first. Only God should be first before them. The key is, do the latter and it will directly and positively affect the relationship. Don't ask or expect the Lord to bless your marriage and your family, if you are not willing to accept His Son, live for Him, and bring your children up in the "nurture and admonition of the Lord." (Ephesians 6:4)

I am aware that the year is 2025 and that the world has changed, our nation has changed. Along with this evolving cultural transition, has come a desensitization to sin. So much so, that an attitude has developed among many that really sin is outdated and that God is old and outdated. If one wants to do something, do it. God is a God of love, and He sends no one to hell (and some don't even believe in hell). God is truly a God of love, grace, mercy, and forgiveness. Going to hell is totally the decision of the individual. The Bible makes it clear that it's His will that "none should perish." Problem is in refusing to believe the Book in its entirety. Since the transgression in the Garden of Eden it has been necessary to accept God's Son. In the Old Testament it was a matter of looking forward to the cross (through animal sacrifices). We look back at the cross for our salvation. Jesus did suffer, die, shoulder sin of all time, and rise again. The cross is the pivotal act and the pivotal point in history. No one makes Heaven without believing and accepting what took place at Calvary. It's not complicated. Jesus is the way, the only way!

We all have opinions, and everyone doesn't interpret Scripture the same. Some things, however, are black and white. They are not up for debate. The best interpreter of Scripture is Scripture. If God's Word says it, I believe it. I have staked both my life and death on its truth.

I am fully aware of "live and let live," as well as "if it feels good, do it." In His Word the Lord has provided a prescription, a plan, a design by which we are to live. Ignoring that doesn't make it disappear. Yes, the world has changed. Yes, the culture has changed. The Lord? "Jesus Christ the same yesterday, and today; and forever" (Hebrews 13:8). Proverbs 14:12 says, "There is a way that seemeth right unto a man, but the end thereof are the ways of death." The New International Version (NIV) states it this way, "There is a way that appears to be right, but in the end it leads to death."

I am going to preface what I will say next with this: I love the Lord. I love all people, including folks of any color, any background, any station in life, those who choose to forgo God's plan for marriage, those who live alternate lifestyles, the saved and the unsaved. Loving doesn't mean agreeing. I didn't write the Bible, I don't make the rules. I have been called to preach and teach and remind people of what the Word of God says on all matters. I believe, preach, and teach the inspired, inerrant, infallible Word of God. We must be careful when we choose to be "open" when God says it is against His Word. I believe the Word when it says, "...speaking the truth in love" (Ephesians 4:15).

During the years I had a counseling ministry, I had people meet with me who clearly had their own agenda. Whether it met with God's standards or not, they wanted me to endorse their behavior or living situation. Of course, as a Christian\Biblical counselor, I couldn't do that. I emphasized that I could love them, pray for them, even meet with them. At the same time, they were disarming me to help them. Yes, I understood their practical approach regarding their "situation", but it still didn't make it right. For me to call it right would be to do a grave disservice and injustice to them. Some couples would get it and work at turning their circumstances around. Others? Well, they thought I was behind the times and maybe a little crazy. But folks, it is what it is. We have choices to make throughout our lives. We choose to listen to Goliath or to God.

In Jesus' teachings alone, we have before us the standards, the principals, the convictions by which we are to live our lives. People can disagree with me, argue against my position in these matters but at "the end of the day" they don't answer to me but to Him who sits on the throne. If we believe God's Word, then we understand that there is no acceptable substitute for living together as husband and wife, without being husband and wife. Yes, marriage is more than a piece of paper but God sanctions marriage as the arrangement He has provided. Love and commitment should never ignore the Lord's plan of marriage. It is not for me to judge folks in what they are doing. Judgment belongs to the Lord. Of course, it would be remiss on my part to not be obedient to the Word and to take God at His Word. I want to see people blessed and happy. Nothing supersedes God's prescription for that.

Divorce is real. It happens far too frequently, and was never what the Lord intended. He does weigh in about divorce and remarriage. I don't judge folks who divorce or choose to marry again. Still, that doesn't change the teaching of the Bible on those subjects. The Scripture clearly sets forth the criteria. There are plenty of reasons people have for divorcing. I have no difficulty understanding that, in many instances. While not foolproof, my emphasis here is be very careful in choosing a mate for life. If people mess up, is there forgiveness for the transgression? Thanks be to God, yes. Otherwise, we would all be in trouble.

The Bible is clear about marriage. Let's start with Genesis 2:24, "Therefore shall a man leave his father and his mother, and shall cleave unto his wife: and they shall be one flesh." God says to be one flesh, to be intimate, to be sexually engaged is not to be with a friend, a girlfriend, a fiancée — but rather it is to occur only between a man and his wife.

- In Matthew 19:2, Jesus repeats Genesis 2:24. His teaching, His emphasis once again is between only husband and wife.
- 1 Corinthians 7:2, Paul teaches, "…to avoid fornication, let every man have his own wife, and let every woman have her own husband." The Greek of the New Testament renders the word fornication as applying to relationships that involve sexual activity, that is outside the parameters of God. It covers a plethora of sexual sins, including sex before marriage, prostitution, incest, homosexuality. There are other Scriptures that address all these things that are not in the will of God. Some examples are as follows.
- Galatians 5:19-21 addresses the "works of the

flesh." Among those listed are fornication and adultery.

- Ephesians 5:3, Paul is writing to the church at Ephesus. He makes the point fornication should "not once be named among you."
- Hebrews 13:4 says that "Marriage is honourable in all…"

Again, there is much more information in the Word about marriage, divorce, remarriage. My point is simply that God has not given us the prerogative to change or update His Word. Revisions may be appropriate in many areas in our culture, but the Bible is to be untouched.

Maybe right here would be a good place to include some tips for a good marriage. No guarantee but worth a try. The information here is not intended to be exhaustive or complete but just some things I'm sharing from my personal experience and from my heart. I know I have gone a long way around the barn to get to some other points I want to make. As a seed to launch us into some simple and basic tips/truths about having a successful marriage, I want to start with Ecclesiastes 4:9, "Two are better than one."

1. It is no longer about just "me." Marriage is a partnership, a contract, a companionship. Putting someone else first is not a bad thing. In fact, it is rewarding. I like receiving and I am always grateful when someone gifts me with something. But when the Bible states, "it is more blessed to give than to receive" (Acts 20:35). These are the words of Jesus. It is "dead on." I have found giving to be far more rewarding than receiving. What better place for that to happen than within the bonds of marriage.

2. Put God first. There is no substitute for this action. Fail to do it and do not expect the Lord to bless your union. Your spouse deserves that. So do kids that will bless the marriage. When I was in the Holy Land many years ago, I had the honor of standing at the location where Jesus preached the powerful Sermon on the Mount. I was further blessed to read aloud a portion of that sermon to our listeners. As recorded in Matthew 6:33, these are some of the words that fell from His lips in that sermon, "But seek ye first the kingdom of God, and his righteousness; and all these things shall be added to you."

3. Build a home together. Before we were married, I had lived in at least 11 different houses (this includes my college dormitory). Carol lived in 4

different houses. When we married, one of our goals was to someday have a home of our own. That took a while. We did not have our own home built until 12 years after we were married. I pastored churches and we moved around some. We lived in parsonages and rentals. We lived in 9 different houses. When we moved into our own home, it was number 10. Thankfully, we lived there for 42.5 years. As we aged and good health was beginning to elude us, we moved to a standalone apartment in the same town, Mt. Vernon. It is an apartment owned by Son Matt and Holly. We sold our house that we loved up on the hill and in the woods. About a year and a half after moving to the apartment (that we called our cabin), Carol went to her home with Jesus. I am still living here. Now, it has been a total of a little over four years (at the time of this writing). My point is this. We lived in lots of places, including several different towns. It did not take us having a house built to have a home. Our home was wherever we were and wherever our kids were. Don't worry about where you live but how you live. Remember, a house never built a home. We loved our house on the hill and in the woods. We loved the location and the privacy. We loved our neighbors. Carol picked out the house plan. She and I both made some revisions in the plan to better suit what we wanted.

4. Love each other with your whole heart, your whole being. No matter how short or long time you have been married, your love should never change. If there is a change, it should be that love continues to grow deeper.

5. Faithfulness is imperative. I know people mess up and get entangled in other relationships (affairs) even though they are married. Of course, the Bible is clear regarding any kind of fornication or adultery. First and foremost, walk with the Lord, stay in His Word to prevent such actions. If it does happen, yes God will forgive. Hopefully, so will the offended spouse. It is not wise to depend on that. Commitment, which is cardinal in marriage, is not based on convenience or feelings. If we marry someone, we need to be committed from the wedding day "until death do us part."

6. Another characteristic of marriage should be transparency. Be honest with one another. Communicate with one another. We should be fully trustworthy. We want to trust our spouse. Our spouse conversely should be able to trust us.

7. Forgiveness is necessary. Where there are two imperfect people, there will always be times that

forgiving one another is crucial.

8. After God, put your sweetheart and family first. Yes, in the age in which we live, this is not easy. Work, career, profession, other interests — nothing is more important than our nuclear family.

9. Even when children come along don't stop being a couple. There is room for both.

Much is taught about these matters in God's Word. Just one example I would call your attention to is Ephesians 5:22-33. This passage is a wonderful standard bearer for marriage. Take time to read it or read it again. Do so prayerfully, asking the Lord to impress its truth into the depths of your heart. The roles for marriage in the passage should leave no doubt relative to what our relationship should be.

Most marriages don't fit the idea of Camelot. Former First Lady Jacqueline Kennedy (later Onassis) depicted her husband's administration as the "American Camelot." There are those who perceived their marriage to be the same. I'll leave the reader here to draw your own conclusion about that. The truth is that Camelot is fictional. Beware of folks who tell you about their perfect marriage. People who claim their marriage is perfect, or that they are perfect, frighten me.

Guys and Gals, I fully understand the lack of perfection in a marriage between two imperfect people. That is a given. However, please make it the priority it should be. If you fail, immediately seek God's forgiveness. It is the only resolution.

Chapter 6
Dispatching Goliath from Our Family

The Book of Genesis reveals the "beginning" of numerous things, not the least of which is the family. After creating "man" and "woman" (Adam and Eve), it wasn't long until they birthed children. God created their children but chose the couple as vessels of their physical birth.

One of the greatest desires Carol and I had was to marry one another, knowing the Lord was orchestrating that union. Secondly, it was our desire to fill our quiver with children. God blessed our marriage with four children (2 daughters and 2 sons). At the time of this writing, their ages are Melissa Anne, age 60; Michael Wayne II, age 58; Marla Jo, age 54; and Matthew Jason, age 51. Their mom called them her trophies. Same for me. Our kids are a gift, a blessing, a joy. Psalm 127:3 says, "...children are an heritage of the Lord..." I am humbled and grateful to the Lord for adding the pleasure of our four. Our kids aren't perfect, nor are they any better or worse than others. Behaviors may be different. Character may be different. Opportunities may be different. However, in terms of value we all are special to the Lord. After all, the Father sent His Son to the cross for everyone who has ever been born or ever will be born. The ground at the cross is level.

During the years our youngsters were growing up we had a full house. Parenting isn't easy. Most of us learn how to parent by practicing on our kids. I do miss those days of when they were little. We engaged in so many activities and had so much fun. Of course, as they got older sports came, driving came, dating time came, eventually marriage, etc. Speaking of sports, among our four were baseball, football, basketball, cheerleading, tennis, golf, camping, hiking, backpacking, hunting, fishing, martial arts. I likely have missed some. I ate enough Big Mac's after games that my middle name should be Mac.

Holidays were always so special. Even to this day I can smell the turkey or ham that Carol was preparing. There were birthdays — quite a few in a family our size.

The most important thing we could have ever done for our children was to raise them in church and lead them to the Lord. I was not only their dad but their pastor many of those years. Their mom and I led them to the Lord. I baptized all of them and performed the wedding ceremonies for all of them. What a blessing for dad. Later, in stages they grew up, graduated high school, went off to college, and found their soulmates. So, our family grew. What an added blessing for us — two wonderful sons-in-law and two wonderful daughters-in-law joining our family. Jon Stewart, Rhonda Reid Bryant, Todd Hart, and Holly Weaver Bryant brought joy to our family unit. We also have a good relationship with their families and our kids' in-laws.

Melissa and Jon have now been married for 38 years. Jon is the CEO of his company and Melissa is an attorney. Jon is a graduate of Ohio State University. Melissa is a graduate of the University of the Cumberlands and the Ohio State Michael E. Motitz College of Law. They have our Grandson Jon Hunter (Hunter) and Granddaughter Carol Anne (Annie). They also have our first Great Grandson Thomas Owens Stewart (Hunter & Katherine).

Michael and Rhonda have now been married for

33 years. Michael is the vice president of his company and Rhonda has taught high school English for several years. The last few years she has served in a specialty position that involves training educators, etc. Michael is a graduate of Union Commonwealth University. Rhonda has an under graduate degree from the University of the Cumberlands and a Master's in Education from Eastern Kentucky University. They have our Grandsons Trey (Michael Wayne III), William Andrew and Reid Elizabeth.

Marla and Todd have been married for 23 years. Marla is a medical transcriptionist and Todd is a communications engineer. Marla attended both the University of the Cumberlands and Eastern Kentucky University. They have our Grandsons Hunter Todd, Mackenzie (Mac) and Gable Grey. They also have our Great Granddaughter Josie Quinn (Hunter & Katie).

Matthew and Holly have been married for 27 years. Matt is a Detective Lieutenant over the Criminal Investigation Department (CID) with the Pulaski County Sheriff's Office and Holly is a 3rd grade teacher at Brodhead Elementary. Matt has an under graduate degree in business from the University of the Cumberlands and has a Master's in Criminal Justice, also from the University of the

Cumberlands. He is a graduate of the Criminal Justice Academy, where he completed his law enforcement training, and finished first in his class. In high school he was a Governor's Scholar at Centre College. Holly has both her undergraduate and Master's in Education from the University of the Cumberlands. Her Master's degree includes a dual emphasis in elementary education and special education. They have our Grandsons Matthew Grant (Grant), Garrett Jackson, Sawyer Quinn, and Lincoln Wyatt.

My Christmas and birthday list has grown exponentially *LOL*. Counting the kids, their spouses, the grandkids, their spouses, and the great grandkids — I am up to 26 on my list but I love it.

Carol has not met our great grandkids. She will. As the hymn says, "What a day that will be." Also, who knows? She may already be aware of them. It would add to her joy in Heaven. What those people may know who have gone on before us has been a centuries-long debate. Some believe the soul sleeps till the rapture. Others believe those who have passed over are aware of at least some things. There are a few Scriptures that support that understanding. The bottom line is that none of us know for sure. However, God is doing it the way it is supposed to be. For me? Well, I talk to Carol every day.

I don't know what she sees, hears, or knows. I just know that she lives in my heart and that I feel her presence. In my small apartment there are at least 50 pictures on display of her. I sleep on her side of the bed, on the same mattress, and on her pillow. Folks can say they want but it all brings me comfort. I continue to dream about her at night. It's kind of a way that I still have her here.

Back to our family. I am so proud of our offspring (as was Carol). In terms of not being addicted to drugs, not been in jail, success with their education, career, profession, and family — well, how can I not be thankful. I live right behind Matt's and Holly's in their apartment. Melissa and Marla and their families live in Lexington. Michael and his family live in Corbin. I am about the same distance from them, south and north of me. I am sort of in a hub between them, geographically. Most importantly is the spiritual legacy their mom and I are leaving for them, and the spiritual walk and focus for their own lives. No matter what they achieve in life, in terms of their education, their professions and careers, their families, etc. (and I am proud of all of them for those things), nothing will ever be as important to their mom or me than them knowing, walking with, and serving the Lord. What a comfort it is to know that the circle will not be broken!

Our grandkids are a delight. They have all made us so proud and so thankful. The following is what they have done educationally, and are doing in the workplace:

> Grandson Hunter Stewart is a graduate of Vanderbilt University, where he was on the golf team four years. In his senior year he was selected as SEC Player of the Year, the first in Vandy's history. He went on to play professional golf throughout the United States and several countries around the world. He eventually formed his own company and now works with pros on their game. Granddaughter-in-Law Katherine is a graduate of Georgia Southern University and is a graphic designer. The couple live in Atlanta, Georgia with their son, Thomas Owens Stewart.

> Granddaughter Annie Myers is a graduate of Auburn University and holds a Doctor of Juris Prudence from the University of Kentucky J. David Rosenberg College of Law. She is with a law firm in Louisville. Her husband, Cameron, is also a graduate of the University of Kentucky J. David Rosenberg College of Law, with undergraduate and Doctor of Juris Prudence degrees from the University of Kentucky. He is with a different law firm in Louisville. The couple

currently reside in Louisville.

➢ Grandson Trey holds undergraduate and MBA degrees from the University of the Cumberlands. He is an accountant for the company where he works. Granddaughter-in-Law Kamryn holds an undergraduate and a Master's in Counseling, both from the University of the Cumberlands. She works in the Gear Up program for the Williamsburg High School. The couple live in Williamsburg. Trey and Kamryn are both involved with music. Trey is a country music artist, doing vocals and playing several instruments. He and Kamryn travel extensively and play numerous venues. Trey now has an agent. He has a full band, is merchandising and signing autographs for fans. He is also a great songwriter, performing several of the songs he has written. As a Nashville recording artist, he has released several singles.

➢ Grandson William has a degree in psychology from Murray State University and works for an organization in his field. William does vocals and plays various instruments. He has now written several singles and is a Nashville recording artist. Granddaughter-in-Law Mallory has both an undergraduate degree and Master's of Nutrition from Murray State University. She now works for an institution in her field. The couple live in Murray, Ky.

➢ Granddaughter Reid Elizabeth is a freshman at Transylvania University in Lexington. She is also a very talented singer, musician, and songwriter, doing vocals and playing several instruments. She is a Nashville recording artist and has released several singles. Reid was a Governor's Scholar at Centre College. She is a member of the Chi Omega Sorority and is also elected as a Senator for the Transylvania University Student Government Association. Reid and Annie are our two granddaughters. The other ten are of the male species.

➢ Grandson Hunter Hart is the sales manager at Dan Cummins Auto Dealership in Paris, Kentucky. He attended Eastern Kentucky University. He is our super salesman. Granddaughter-in-Law Katie is a Certified Pharmacy Tech at the University of Kentucky. They live in Paris with their daughter, Josie Quinn Hart.

➢ Grandson Mac lives in Lexington. He is a bank officer and has a degree in mathematics from Centre College.

➢ Grandson Gable is a junior at Tates Creek High School in Lexington. He has played baseball since he was very young. He now pitches for the

Lexington Tates Creek High School team and plays other summer and early fall leagues. He plans to attend college and is already being contacted by some prestigious universities based on his academic standing and his potential to play baseball for them. He will likely go the route of math and science. He is interested in medical school.

➤ Grandson Grant is a graduate of the University of the Cumberlands and the Kentucky Department of Criminal Justice and finished first in his academy class. He is a deputy with the Pulaski County Sheriff's Office. He is also a tournament bass fisherman. This past year, his first year with his agency, he was chosen as Deputy of the Year and received an award for valor. He lives in his own apartment in Mt. Vernon.

➤ Grandson Garrett is a student at Somerset Community College (an affiliate of the University of Kentucky). He works at Save A Lot. He, too, is a musical guy. He has his own band and does vocals and plays guitar. He and his girlfriend, Ellie, became an item in 7th grade and still are. Garrett is 20 and lives at home in Mt. Vernon.

➤ Grandson Twin Sawyer and Grandson Twin Lincoln are eight graders this year (2025). They love to swim. The pool here is right behind their house and my apartment. They are also members of the Rockcastle County Schools Bass Fishing Team. Their dad, who for a few years was the coach of the high school bass fishing team, is their boat captain.

For about six years some of our family participated in Civil War reenactment. Matt and I rode cavalry. Michael was on a cannon crew. Later, Matt, his family, Carol and I became Colonial/18th century reenactors. That was for around six years, too. After being out of the hobby for several years, Matt, Holly, Garrett, the Twins, and I jumped back into 18th century reenacting during 2025. I continue with my long hunter impression, while Matt performs as William Whitley and Joseph Martin.

I have plenty of regrets as I look back on my life. How I long to have do overs. Yet, one regret I don't have is spending time with my kids and grandkids. The years of hunting, fishing, camping, backpacking, hiking, canoeing, horses, reenactments, martial arts, picnics, traveling have meant everything to me. For me, most of my activities are in the past. Although, I am known to do a little hunting and fishing, and of course the reenactments. Last season (2024) I harvested an eight-point buck and a grey fox. As Son Michael says, "Dad's still a shooter."

LOL. As a gun and knife enthusiast, I have been known to collect a few. And, cabin life? Oh yeah! Carol and I built a somewhat rustic home in the woods, where we lived for over 42 years. We both liked the Adirondack look and built our home that way and decorated accordingly. My living room in the apartment where I am now is cabin style. My bedroom with a log bed and cowboy décor provide the feeling that I'm on the range. In my mind I have been a cowboy since I was 4 years old. I never got over it. Matt and I kept and rode horses for years, as did Michael. In fact, Michael has horses now. Matt and I used them in reenactments, but many times simply cowboyed up. I would share how many western hats, boots, shirts, jeans, jackets, guns, knives I have but it would be embarrassing. I am blessed to be involved in the Cowboy Church in our county. I am a member of and attend Bible Baptist Church here in Mt. Vernon. However, one Sunday a month I attend and try to lend some support to the Cowboy Church. It is a local outreach for me. Pastor Rex Williams does a terrific job of leading that congregation. He is quite the cowboy and muleskinner himself. Our Pastor Alan Dotson and Associate Pastor Justin at Bible Baptist bless us with their leadership.

Among other family are our nieces and

nephews. There are four on my side (my sister's kids), and five on Carol's side (her 3 sisters). My sister's offspring are Carey, Genene, Tracy, and April. Carey, Genene, Tracy all live in Michigan. April lives in Arizona. Carol's sisters' offspring are Diana, David, and Debbie, all in Michigan. Cindy lives in Texas. Rob, who lived in Oklahoma, died a few years ago. Then there is Richard, who I believe is in California, Michele, who lives in New Jersey. Randy lives in Arizona, and Janet lives in Michigan. It would be difficult to name all my great nieces and nephews, but all our family thinks of one great niece as a special young lady. Breanna has had challenges to face since birth but is such a sweetheart who loves Jesus and makes everyday a full and happy one.

Although not officially family, I have some folks in my circle who are like family. Casey McClure is the Park Manager at Wilderness Road State Park in Virginia and Liz is a probation & parole officer; Nathaniel Price is a Chief of Police, Roy Martin owns Dowell & Martin Funeral Home, along with his wife Pam, who also owns Sparks Flowers & More here in Mt. Vernon; John Nugent owns his own business and his wife Barb is an educator in the public school; Mike and Pam Durham are good friends who live here in Mt. Vernon. Mike is one of my former karate instructors. Don Moreland is someone I have known for forty-eight years. He and I have always been close. I helped conduct his wife's funeral. We were neighbors for almost 43 years. He is a remarkable gentleman, a fine Christian man. As l write this, he is less than a month from being 99 years of age. What an inspiration he is. There are so many who could be named but I would likely at best leave some out. These folks are from my past pastorates, church memberships, from the various communities where we lived over the years, my classmates from Clinton High School, friends and past fellow students during my college years, my current community and current church family, Phillip Payne, the late Vall Franklin, the late Ott Bond, and the late Dean Carpenter. I would like to name them all. However, to do would be a volume of its own. Ministerial mentors Edgar Owens, Seal Janeway, and Raymond Lawrence are folks I am very indebted to for pouring into my life when I was a young minister. A special minister friend, Randy McPheron, has meant much to me during the past several years. Former Pastors Mark Harrell and Travis Gilbert, Bruce Ross, Jack Bruce, as well as the late Dr. Charles Hedrick have all been a significant influence in my life. Also Gerald Manchester, Albert Liford, and Jack Weaver.

One person I want to especially mention is Lloyd Bennett. I met Lloyd when he was a boy at a church I pastored many years ago. He is the same age as our oldest daughter. Lloyd and Lisa did much of the ground work during my three campaigns for mayor. Especially since Carol has been gone, Lloyd has become my best friend. He frequently calls and checks on me. He and I spend time eating out, going to Walmart, gun shops, auctions, rodeos, etc. He also goes with me to the Cowboy Church. Due to my poor health, I sometimes need someone to accompany me to appointments. Lloyd is disabled and has his own issues but is always willing to step up when needed. Of course, if he needs me, I am glad to reciprocate.

To wrap up this chapter on family I want to share some last thoughts and mention some Scriptures that I think is helpful as we consider the family. As it is with marriage, having a family and rearing a family are not exactly easy. In fact, at times it can be quite challenging. One of my primary goals over the years was to be a good husband and a good dad. I think (hope) I did a decent job, yet I know there are things I could have done better. I am grateful that our family remains compatible and close. I feel for and care about families who are broken and sometimes devastated by their experiences in marriage and family. I am a "bleeding heart" when it comes to wanting the best for other folks. I have tried to step up through ministry, social work, law enforcement, politics, and contract programs to do just that. At best, sometimes there are limitations as to what we can do to help. We clearly should never cease to pray for others, no matter the circumstances.

Here are some Scriptures that will both encourage and challenge us:

- Psalm 127:3-5, "...children are an heritage of the Lord; ...As arrows are in the hand of a mighty man; so are children of thy youth. Happy is the man that hath his quiver full of them..."
- Proverbs 22:6, "Train up a child in the way he should go: and when he is old, he will not depart from it."
- Proverbs 19:17, "Correct thy son, and he shall give thee rest; yea, he shall give delight unto thy soul."
- Proverbs 17:6, "Children's children are the crown of old men; and the glory of the children are their fathers." The New International Version (NIV) says it this way, "Children's

children are a crown to the aged, and parents are the pride of their children." This is a dual matter of grandkids honoring their elders and it provides the avenue for us older folks to be proud of them.

- Ephesians 6:4, "…ye fathers, provoke not your children to wrath: but bring them up in the nurture and admonition of the Lord." The bottom line here is whatever we do regarding our children should be loving, caring, and what's in their best interest. Discipline is necessary. The Bible teaches that. Instruction, discipline yes. Abuse, absolutely not! Colossians 3:21 renders something similar.

- 1 Timothy 5:8, "But if any provide not for his own, and specifically for those of his own house, he hath denied the faith, and is worse than an infidel." Wow! This one has a serious tone with a serious consequence if not heeded. What does it mean to provide for our family. Some of the obvious things are food, shelter, clothing, health care, education, etc. Clearly it would also include protection. What parent would not be willing to protect their loved ones. When I say what I am about to say, some will be turned off. As a conservative, a patriot, and as a pro gun guy, I believe in self-defense. God honors it, as do the laws in every state. I know it varies from state to state but there is a provision all around our country. We have a military that protects us against all enemies, foreign and domestic. We have law enforcement that looks out for us on the local level. I wholeheartedly support both our military and our law enforcement officers. We should thank God every day for those who put their lives on the line for us. Yet, at the end of the day, there are times and situations where we can only depend on ourselves. I don't apologize for being a card-carrying NRA member for many years. I am not "trigger happy." I have spent my entire adult life trying to help people, not harm them. Obviously, lethal force is a last resort. However, when it comes to protecting my family, to the best of my ability I will do everything in my power to do so. I find that most people who are anti-gun, are those who have never been in a survival situation. Although it is a whole different subject, I feel the same about abortion. I am on the same page as former President Ronald Reagan, when he said about abortion, "I've noticed that everyone who is for abortion has already been born."

I want to say something here (once again some folks will disagree with me). Before I share that information, I want to remind you that God loves everyone, and so does Mike Bryant. Praying for everyone is both a duty and a delight.

As a Christian, a minister, a conservative — my stand has been known for years by those who know me. I don't believe in abortion, I don't believe in homosexuality, I don't believe in transgenderism, I don't believe in the practice of transvestites. I believe God made Adam and Eve, not Adam and Steve. When God creates a life, He makes no mistake. There is a purpose. To me, it is a fearful thing to end a life (which I believe begins at inception). Murdering in the womb or outside of the womb, murdering a child, murdering a young person, or murdering an adult — to God it's still murder. In terms of alternate lifestyles, we all have a choice about those decisions. Just because our culture espouses such behaviors does not mean that God approves. And, folks, if God disapproves, who am I to embrace anything different to His will? Again, I love all these people, I pray for them, and I will be kind to them. However, my mandate is to preach the truth of God's Word. I think Galatians 1:8-10 says it best, "But though we, or an angel from heaven, preach any other gospel unto you than that which we have preached unto you, let him be accursed. As we said before, so say I now again, If any man preach any other gospel unto you than that ye have received, let him be accursed. For do I now persuade men, or God? Or do I seek to please men? For if I yet pleased men, I should not be the servant of Christ."

Some would likely ridicule me, call me an old fogie, say I am not with it, or whatever. That's okay. I believe in freedom of speech. You know, not one person will answer to me, and I will answer to no one. All of us will stand before the Lord sometime soon to give an account to the rightful Judge. There will be no "innocent until proven guilty" and no defense attorney. Excuses and explanations for choosing wrong over right will be wasted breath. Do we want to hear Him say "depart from me for I never knew you" or "well done thou good and faithful servant?" Which one do you think Goliath wants you to hear? It is time for some sober thinking here. The world says do whatever you want but God says listen to His voice. As human beings, do we know that we can die within one heartbeat/one breath? My counsel would be let's all make sure we are on God's side. I can't choose for you. God won't choose for you. What's it going to be? Embrace Goliath or surrender all to Christ? I judge no one. Judgment belongs to God. Psalm 75:7, "But God is the judge." Isaiah 33:22, "For the Lord is our judge..." Ecclesiastes 12:14, "For God shall bring every work into judgment, with every secret thing, whether it be good, or whether it be evil."

Here are some more Scriptures that address that which I have mentioned. Why do I take the stand I do? It is what God's Word teaches.

- Psalm 139:13-16, "For you created my inmost being; you knit me together in my mother's womb. I praise you because I am fearfully and wonderfully made; your works are wonderful, I know that full well. My frame was not hidden from you when I was made in the secret place, when I was woven together in the depths of the earth. Your eyes saw my unformed body; all the days ordained for me were written in your book before one of them came to be."

- Leviticus 18:22, "Thou shalt not lie with mankind, as with womankind: it is abomination."

- Leviticus 20:13, "If a man also lie with mankind, as he lieth with a woman, both of them have committed an abomination: they shall surely be put to death; their blood shall be upon them."

- Romans 1:26-27, "For this cause God gave them

up unto vile affections: for even their women did change the natural use into that which is against nature. And likewise also the men, leaving the natural use of the woman, burned in their lust one toward another; men with men working that which is unseemly, and receiving in themselves that recompence of their error which was meet."

- 1 Corinthians :9-10, "Know ye not that the unrighteous shall not inherit the kingdom of God? Be not deceived: neither fornicators, nor idolaters, nor adulterers, nor effeminate, nor abusers of themselves with mankind. Nor thieves, nor covetous, nor drunkards, nor revilers, nor extortioners, shall inherit the kingdom of God."

- Deuteronomy 22:5, "The woman shall not wear that which pertaineth unto a man, neither shall a man put on a woman's garment: for all that do so are abomination unto the Lord thy God."

Chapter 7
Dispatching Goliath from Our Personal Journey
Regardless of the Thistles and Thorns

Psalm 139:14 tells us, "I will praise thee; for I am fearfully and wonderfully made: marvelous are thy works; and that my soul knoweth right well." The New King James Version (NKJV) states it this way, "I praise you because I am fearfully and wonderfully made; your works are wonderful, I know that full well."

In his creative genius God uniquely made everyone that has ever been born or ever will be born. We are who we are and like no one else. Among the billions of people no two people have the same fingerprints. Only God does that! Who then is special? There is an old saying that "God made no junk."

YOU are special in His eyes. He loves every person that He has ever created. When things got messed up in the Garden of Eden, He quickly developed a way of escape, a rescue operation. It involves the need to be recreated. 2 Corinthians 5:17 clarifies this, "Therefore if any man be in Christ, he is a new creature: old things are passed away; behold, all things are become new." The Living Bible (TLB) paraphrase puts it this way, "When someone becomes a Christian, he becomes a new person inside. He is not the same anymore. A new life has begun."

While becoming a new person does not mean that we are pure or perfect, a significant change occurs. Our heart is never the same. When we do "miss the mark" our conscience immediately engages, our conviction is more poignant. In fact, the only way we can be prepared for Heaven is to be clothed in His righteousness. When I was young and not walking with the Lord as I should have, anything I did that was not in the will of the Father was something that strongly convicted me. It was only when I became penitent before Him and sought His forgiveness that I could have His joy again. I accepted the Lord and came into relationship with Him when I was twelve. So, was the relationship terminated when I sinned? Let me put it this way. Once we have been introduced to someone, we know them. We can't "unmeet" them. That never changes. When we receive Christ as our Savior we are being introduced to Him. We have not stopped being believers. Then, what happens? Our fellowship can be severed, which will leave us in a miserable predicament until we have that restored. I suppose the most famous Scripture we reference regarding restoration is in Psalm 51. King David knew the Lord. He was a man after God's own heart. Yet, he committed grievous sins of adultery and murder. His famous Psalm does not reflect him asking to know God again but to restore the joy he had lost. A person who is truly born again will not be happy but rather miserable when they sin. That's the Lord's pull on us. One of the functions of the Holy Spirit (the 3rd person of the Godhead) is to convict of sin (John 16:8). Years ago, a minister who was one of my mentors put it this way, "God is not an Indian giver." Here is the problem with falling from grace. Which sin causes the fall? Does it mean things such as murder, stealing, etc. Does it mean we simply failed to do something the Lord wanted us to do (sin of omission)? Since we are not sinless and since we are sinners after we are saved (sinners saved by grace), it would seem we would need to be saved every day or perhaps every minute. I love and respect my fellow believers (some of whom are dear friends) who believe that we are saved by grace through faith—and works. Ephesians speaks loudly and clearly when it says in Ephesians 2:8-9, "For by grace are ye saved through faith; and that not of yourselves: it is the gift of God: Not of works, lest any man should boast." In the New Testament the Pharisees were notorious for tooting their own horn. Their self-righteous, pious, condescending attitude didn't set well with Jesus. He found it very repugnant. Jesus pointed out to them that instead of being so busy wiping off the outside of the cup they might want to clean up the filth on the inside of the cup. We can work our fingers "to the bone" and it could never be enough to make us worthy of the Lord or Heaven. "Good enough" is nonexistent. Jonathan Ewards, the 18th century Congregational minister and philosopher, said it well, "You contribute nothing to your salvation except the sin that made it necessary."

For one, I am thankful that my entering Heaven is not dependent on how many things I can try to impress the Lord with. Also, He knows our nature. Next thing is we would be as the Pharisees—bragging on all the good stuff we have done. Now, please don't misunderstand. It is not wrong to do good works for the Lord. We need to follow the teachings of Scripture and be obedient. In the same passage in Ephesians 2 the very next verse speaks of our workmanship. We need to be busy about our "Father's business." Other places in the Bible reveal to us that we are rewarded based on what we do in our bodies. The Lord, in His usual generosity, provides bonuses. Don't let up. Don't quit working. Not to mention, I can't think of anything that brings us more joy here on earth than serving the Lord. In God's eyes faithfulness and obedience are preeminent. Many years ago, I heard someone preaching and he said something to this effect, "You can't spell God without go, you can't spell good without go, and you can't spell gospel without go." Keep going for the Lord. Don't let up. Don't slow down. Keep the pedal to the metal. That's how soul winning happens. A simple example of how our God saves and keeps us is with my father. There were many times I displeased him. Sometimes discipline was required. Just as our Heavenly Father who disciplines us because He loves us, the same with my earthly father. There were times I "fell out of fellowship" with my dad but he never stopped being my father and there was never a need to meet him again. I have always known him and always will.

I strongly believe in accepting the Lord as Savior. I very much believe in following the Lord in baptism (by immersion). The Greek word for baptism is *baptizo*, which means to immerse. I am acutely aware of some faiths that baptize by other methods, namely sprinkling and pouring. I am not criticizing them or judging them. I love them. I am just providing the biblical definition. Of the numerous baptisms I have done over the years, there is only one time I did it differently. The lady had accepted the Lord and wanted to be baptized. This was not long before she died. She was in no way physically able to be immersed. I agreed to pour the water over her. For what it is worth, I soaked her whole body. Let's not get so legalistic that we are unreasonable. Also, as important as baptism is, and it is commanded by our Lord, no one should delude themselves into believing that baptism, church membership, regular church attendance, being good to people, involvement in community affairs, being good to one's family, etc., etc. are at all sufficient for entry into Heaven. Glad the thief on the cross wasn't dependent on any of that, because he had not done any of that. Yet, Jesus promised Him immediate entrance into Paradise just before the thief died. That was a classic case of "deathbed repentance." Please don't wait for that opportunity because it may never happen. It is a very slender plank upon which to depend.

The chapter title here includes thistles and

thorns. Many of us are all too acquainted with Goliath putting obstacles in our path. There is no doubt that he plants land mines all along the road of our life's journey. He loves to attack our serving the Lord, our marriages, our families, our work, our everything and anything that is good and Godly. Remember, he doesn't rest, he doesn't sleep.

When I look at my life, I have seen him rear his ugly head way too often. He is merciless. He is ruthless. His egregious behavior is over the top. His relentless assaults remind us of why it is necessary every minute of every day and night to wear the "whole amor of God." Goliath had his armor on the day David terminated/dispatched him. It is true that David declined to wear armor that day but realistically he was wearing armor. He was wearing the only armor that works. No, it isn't visible to the naked eye, but it is the best protection available. God furnishes our armor. He even provides the stone and the sling. The Apostle Paul explains what it is in Ephesians 6:10-18. Here is what we need to put on every day. The belt of truth, breastplate of righteousness, shoes of the gospel of peace, shield of faith, helmet of salvation, and carry the sword of the Spirit. Let Goliath's fiery darts assail. It won't matter. God has got this. Anytime we decide to take on Goliath on our own is when we are begging to be defeated. Folks don't do it. You can't win. He is too big, too powerful for us. I will remind you again, "Greater is He who is within us than He who is in the world." (1 John 4:4) Aren't you glad the Lord shows us how to live in victory?

When I was a boy life seemed so simple. I really had few to no responsibilities. My biggest concern was what I would buy with my dime come Saturday. Of course, as the years go by (quite quickly), changes occur, school, chores, and other responsibilities come into play. Then, suddenly (or so it seems) we are grown up. We are focused on work, maybe higher education, getting married, having a family. That sure "ain't" when things get easier.

Once I got my ministry off the ground, I was so excited. I was ready to hit the ground running. Time to prepare to save the world. While I was growing up in the evangelical church I was somewhat aware of problems that arose among the parishioners. That would not happen to me. I was "on fire" for the Lord and surely any church and any church member would see that. I would always have their love, respect, and support. Okay, so I was delusional. Little did I know how many thistles and thorns there would be. During the many years I hunted and kept horses, I learned that no matter how much I tried to be careful when I was near a barbed wire fence, or climb over, or crawl under one—I got more than my share of scrapes and cuts. Life's journey is no different. No matter how much we prepare, avoid, or use extreme caution there will be those times of contacting some barbed wire. Goliath has strung it everywhere. I learned over these many ministerial years that church members are interesting. I love church members more than I can say. They have blessed my life. However, a disgruntled church member out of step with the Lord is miserable and they tend to make those around them miserable. They can be the most vicious, malicious, vindictive, merciless, pernicious, bitter, unpleasant, virulent people on earth. I know. I have been the victim of such venom. Having lost their own joy, they will try to rob others of their joy.

There are three songs I have requested at my funeral. They are "Through it All," "Here We Are," and "Rise Again." I have requested these because they have proven to be wonderful worship songs in my life. Also, because they are somewhat descriptive of my life's journey. "Through It All" was written by Andrae' Crouch, a gospel singer, composer, and pastor (1971). It was very personal to him. It reflects some of his own hardships and carries a profound message about faith and reliance on God, especially during difficult times.

So, I went off to college to better prepare for the ministry to which God had called me. I wasn't sure if the Lord had chosen me as another of His vessels to enter the pastorate, do evangelism, become a missionary. I just knew He had called me to preach. I simply lacked the empirical data to know what was next. Better said, I did not know where the Holy Spirit would lead me. I just knew I wanted to move in His anointing, win people to Christ, and serve the Body of Christ.

Professionally, I realized that it was now my career path. I started out preaching but envisioned serving in positions to which the Lord would call me in the work of the Kingdom. I would be added to the long list of clergy, reverends, brothers. As soon as I moved into the dorm at Cumberland College (later to become the University of the Cumberlands), my feet hit the ground running. I met my two roommates, began classes, and adjusted to being away from home and engaged in campus life. One of my roommates, Phillip McClendon, was a ministerial student from Missouri. Later he would be the best man at my wedding. Honestly, it was challenging. Like I said before, no one in my family had gone to college. Academically, I was a good student in high school and obviously I met the requirements to be accepted as a student.

Soon after getting settled, meeting with my advisor, arranging my schedule of classes, things were underway. I also began ministering from the beginning. I became a member of the campus ministerial association and Baptist Student Union (BSU) and participated in teaching the Sunday School lesson on Sunday mornings at a local radio station. I began getting invitations to preach at various churches in the area. I was excited, thankful, and humbled that God was opening doors.

Carol and I married in April before I finished my freshman year in May. We lived off campus in a small mobile home. It sufficed but it wasn't very comfortable. With no shade trees and no air conditioning, and the trailer in the baking sun—it was sweltering in the summer. I continued working at the college's public relations department, and Carol began working in the office of a local physician in Williamsburg, Dr. Bunch. Our parents, although limited, tried to help financially. We lived "close to the bone." Nonetheless, we were happy, and we were all about doing the will of the Lord and doing it together.

That first summer the Carpenter Baptist Church, located sixteen miles from Williamsburg out in the country, called me as their interim pastor for the summer. We just had Sunday school and the morning worship and they paid me $20 per week. That bought our groceries for the week. Families in the church every Sunday took turns taking us to their home after service for a great meal. The congregation was composed of a sweet group of folks. My first pastoral experience was a blessing. When I accepted the pastoral responsibilities, my home church in Michigan ordained me. They had licensed me before I started college. That same week was when I preached a revival meeting for my father-in-law in Ohio.

One of the somewhat unique experiences I had during my first semester with the ministerial association was playing in a football game. The college had an annual football game on Thanksgiving Day. The sporting event took place between the ministerial association and the engineers club. We practiced in the afternoons after classes during September, October, and November. It was a full equipment, full contact game on the gridiron. I played left guard. This was a grown man's game. Both teams consisted of freshmen, sophomores, juniors, and seniors. During the warm-up for the game, I spotted the defensive lineman I would be blocking. He was the biggest player on their team. I was five feet, ten inches and weighed a whopping one-hundred and fifty five pounds. My opponent was my Goliath. Oh well, I was in the best physical shape of my life. I was also taking a PE course in conditioning at that time. Between the practices and the game, a number of us got pretty beat up. We lost that game, but I handled my assignment okay. My big opponent was not as fast as I was. Quick blocks to his knees helped me clear the hole for the runner. He carried a sword and a shield. I carried only a sling shot. *LOL.*

As I was finishing my first semester of my sophomore year, I preached some "trial" sermons for the Southside Baptist Church in Corbin, Kentucky. They called me as pastor. So, we moved from Williamsburg to Corbin (about 16 miles between the two towns) and into the church's parsonage. The pastorium was located next door to the church. Carol no longer worked outside the home but stayed at home and helped me with ministry projects at the church. I traveled back and forth to Williamsburg for classes. I had a good ministry at Southside. Lovely people. Little Daughter Melissa moved into the parsonage with us. The next year our Michael II was born.

After finishing college (I graduated with a Bachelor of Arts with a major in religion and a minor in sociology), the Hyland Heights Baptist Church in Catlettsburg, Kentucky called me as pastor. It is located in the edge of Ashland. From the rental housing the church provided for us we could see the Ohio River with its tugboats. We could also see all three states of Kentucky, Ohio, and West Virginia from our house. It was a different area from what we had been accustomed to. Living in the tri-state area exposed us to even some different beliefs by church members and some cultural differences. While basically subscribing to Southern Baptist doctrine, there were what we thought were some rather bizarre ideas among some of the church members.

Carol and I were young and high energy. When we moved to Catlettsburg, we had our daughter Melissa and our son Michael. The early months of the ministry there were good. The church was located in an industrial area. The church was growing and flourishing. Since the church did not have a parsonage, the church was building a new one. I was so dedicated to the task the Lord had given me — then, enter Goliath! Not unlike the churches in the New Testament era, problems began to surface. Not having faced that before, I tried my best as a young pastor to mediate the situation. Sadly, things just got worse. Eventually, while I enjoyed the support of the majority of the congregation, I decided that it would be better for both the church and my family for me to resign.

We rented a house in Catlettsburg and stayed in the area for several months. After passing the required state insurance exams (life & health) I went to work as a District Agent for Prudential Insurance. I also received invitations from various churches to preach. One of those invitations ended up being a real "barn burner." Richard Chamberlain (not the actor *LOL*), pastor of the Methodist Church in Catlettsburg, asked me to fill the pulpit in his absence. He and his family were going to Nebraska for vacation and he needed me to preach Sunday morning and evening. During the morning worship service at the time the music director (a local attorney) was making some announcements, a man in the back of the church stood up. He was well dressed and articulate. However, he said some things that seemed inappropriate. After he sat down, I didn't think much more about it. After I finished my sermon I offered an invitation for people to come forward to accept the Lord, or for any other prayer needs they might have. Well, this man came forward. He positioned himself directly in front of the platform and podium. He began talking. The organist stopped playing. He looked up at me and said, "I see you have loosened your tie, go ahead and take off your coat." Then he said, "I want us all to go in the back where the Lions Club meets." The music director signaled the organist to begin playing again. The steps to the platform were located at either end of the platform. I saw the gentleman making his way onto the platform to my left. When he got next to me, I said to him, "Brother, will you go back down in front and be in prayer for us. That would really help us." He angrily responded with, "Don't you tell me what to do, I was in the Air Force and I'll throw you right out of here." At that point, the music director came over and got between the man and me. He finally persuaded him to leave the platform. By this time, we just had to end the service in prayer. I went back to the door to greet people as they were leaving. Here comes the man again. He plants himself right in front of me and will not allow people to shake hands with me. My parents, Carol's mom, and one of Carol's sisters were visiting with us that weekend. They were attending the service. All of us were confused about what happened. Our visiting family went back home that afternoon. I wasn't about to take Carol and the kids back with me that night. When I arrived at the church, I was informed that after I left that morning the man beat up one of the teenagers in the church. He went down the street and when he encountered another man, he broke his ribs. Finally, a police officer arrested him. It took six people to get him in cuffs. What caused this man to disrupt the service? He had been under psychiatric care. His psychiatrist was his brother-in-law. He got mad at the brother-in-law and stopped going to see him for treatment and taking the prescribed medications. I found it interesting that the Sunday all of this happened was the man's first time to be in attendance there in twenty-five years. Guess I filled in for Brother Chamberlain in more ways than one. Also, that Sunday night there was a terrible thunderstorm going on. I am sitting on the platform waiting for my time to preach. Next thing I see is the electric going off. They light a couple of candles, but I knew I would not be able to see my Bible or my sermon notes. Just before I approached the podium to hopefully deliver the message, the lights came on again. What a Sunday at the Methodist church that was for me!

After time passed, the Freedom Baptist Church in Mt. Vernon, Kentucky called me as pastor. We loved our days at Freedom. It was out in the country. The parsonage was the old Freedom School house. The church had purchased it and completely renovated it into a house. During our time there, the church built a garage onto the parsonage, bricked everything and did aluminum trim. We went there in 1970 and left there in 1974. It was not a trouble-free ministry. There were some issues that arose that divided the church. It is those problems that often divide churches into church splits. Thankfully, that's not what happened there. My family and I did our best to stay out of the middle and above the fray. Once again, Goliath does what he does. It took a long time for the church to heal in the aftermath of those problems. I am so grateful that Goliath did not get the final blow. Healing and unity came back to the body of Christ in that place. Wonderful people comprised the congregation there. Carol and I felt blessed that we were able to leave there on amicable terms. Some years later I was invited back to speak at a homecoming there.

Feeling a call by the Lord to shift to evangelism, I joined an evangelist and his ministry as an associate evangelist. While preaching in different churches, I also did some front work in locations where the evangelist and our team would conduct tent meetings. Carol and I also opened a Christian bookstore in Corbin, Kentucky, where we once again resided. I helped Carol in the bookstore, but she primarily carried that load. Later, observing some activities that made me feel uncomfortable with the organization, we ended our ministry with the evangelist. For a few weeks I worked at a local church camp helping them clean up following damage from a tornado. First Baptist Church, East Bernstadt, Kentucky called me as pastor. East Bernstadt was one of my better ministries. Loved those congregants. A few years later I moved my family back to Mt. Vernon. That was in 1977. We purchased property and had a house built. We moved into the new house in 1978. We never left Mt. Vernon. Carol was here until she went to Heaven. I am still here. No one knows the future, but I hope I can be here until I join Carol. This is the place where we spent the bulk of our married life, finished raising our kids here, and our youngest son, Matt, and family still live here. It is also where our church is. Bible Baptist Church was the last place Carol and I became members. I still attend and have my membership there. In addition, my parents' and Carol's graves are here. It is where I will be buried. Now, at eighty years of age with multiple health issues, I am for the most part not involved nearly as much in active ministry. I do some things on a limited basis. My health precludes me from doing the ministerial activities I would love to still do. I attend church, occasionally I speak where I am invited, I help with the Cowboy Church. I try to be a witness for the Lord wherever I go. My intention is for this book to minister to people, hopefully long after I have gone to my Heavenly home. Because of the divine call, preachers don't fully retire. However, age and health often dictate one having to step back a bit.

After moving back to Mt. Vernon I passed the required state exam and began working for the Cabinet for Human Resources/Department of Social Services. I was hired as the supervisor for Rockcastle County in 1977 and remained in that position until I retired in 2000. During this same period, I served as interim pastor at Calvary Baptist Church in Corbin, Ky, as well as interim at Fairview Baptist Church and Scaffold Cane Baptist Church, both in Rockcastle County. I was staff evangelist at First Baptist Church, Mt. Vernon four years. I pastored the Scaffold Cane Baptist Church for four years in Rockcastle, County, pastored six years at the Liberty Baptist Church in Pulaski County. Later, I was senior associate pastor at Victory Christian Fellowship in Somerset, and then senior pastor at Faith Harvest Fellowship in Mt. Vernon, which was a work started by my family and me. I was interim pastor at the Buena Vista Baptist Church in Garrard County. The years I was senior associate pastor at Victory Christian Fellowship in Somerset I helped set up the counseling program for all six pastors and was the anchor counselor. In addition, Carol and I led the cell ministry (small groups). We had about 50 groups led by couples in the church.

The work at Faith Harvest Fellowship, for all intents and purposes, was a church. Yet, it had overtones of being a spiritual clinic. Our emphasis was on those unchurched folks, especially those dealing with addictions and other problems. The work was only open for four years but we saw the Lord do so much in the lives of several people. Afterwards we attended church in Mt. Vernon and then back in Somerset.

As part of my life's journey and ministry, the following is a summary of the activities. The intention here is not to brag or complain but to praise the Lord for giving me so many opportunities to serve.

Education & Training

- ➢ Doctor of Ministry (D.Min), International Seminary
- ➢ Master of Theology (TH.M), International Seminary
- ➢ Bachelor of Arts (BA), University of the Cumberlands (Cumberland College)
- ➢ Continuing Education Units:
  - University of Kentucky
  - University of Louisville
  - Eastern Kentucky State University

- Kentucky State University
- University of Iowa
- Spalding University

➢ American Association of Marriage & Family Therapists
➢ Kentucky Department of Mental Health
➢ Smalley Relationship Center
➢ Center for Professional Development
➢ The Ridge Behavioral Center

Other Training

➢ American Association of Christian Counselors Center for Biblical Counseling
➢ Kentucky Department of Criminal Justice Basic Officer Skills Training
➢ Law Enforcement Chemical Weapons Training
➢ Law Enforcement Taser Gun Training
➢ Police Defensive Driving Course Training
➢ Administrative Office of the Courts (AOC) Court Certification Security Training
➢ D.A.R.E. Training in Elementary & Middle School & School Resource Officer, by Kentucky State Police
➢ D.A.R.E. Training for High School, by Tennessee Highway Patrol

- Too Good for Drugs Training by the Kentucky Department of Education School Board Association
- City Official Training (Year 1 and Year 2)

Ministry

- Pastored 6 churches
- Senior Associate Pastor of 1 church
- Interim Pastor of 5 churches
- Staff evangelist of 1 church
- Mission work in Washington D.C., Mexico, Guatemala
- Evangelism
- Preached in 130 different churches in 8 states, Mexico, Guatemala, and Israel — plus schools, colleges, clubs, group homes, abuse shelters, hospitals, nursing homes, church camps, family enrichment retreats, banquets, benefits, memorials, etc.
- Chaplain of Sheriff's Department, 2 Boys Group Homes, Spouse Abuse Shelter
- Laurel Home Guard Civil War Reenactment Chaplain & Cavalry Soldier
- Upper Room Christian Counseling Services Counselor
- Numerous radio & television appearances.

Early morning DJ for gospel music. Hosted 3 of my own radio broadcasts, talk shows, as well as doing high school football radio broadcasts

More
Martial Arts Training (Judo, Shao lin Do Karate, Shotokan Karate, Aki Ju Can Do). Earned black belts in both Shotokan & Aki Ju Can Do. Certified Martial Arts Instructor

Secular Work
(Part Time/Full Time)
Farm work, excavation, dishwasher, factory machine operator, janitor, bottling company, public relations, 3 funeral homes, private security, law enforcement, substitute public school teaching (in 3 school systems), insurance, social worker, social work supervisor, contractor as a Therapeutic Child Support Professional & Alternatives to Detention Case Manager—Mayor of Mt. Vernon for three 4 year terms.

Ministry, Community, Civic, Charitable Memberships
Served in over 100 of these organizations, boards, and committees. Held officer positions in several

of these.

Awards & Honorary Listings, Certifications

Sixteen awards & listings, twenty certifications (Including being made a Lifetime Honorary Member of the Rockcastle County Chamber of Commerce and Inducted into the Republican 5th Congressional District Hall of Fame)

Travel

Forty-six states, Mexico, Guatemala, Greece, Israel, Occupied Syria and Jordan, Canadian Provinces of Ontario, Saskatchewan, Alberta, British Columbia, and the Yukon Territory. Have been as far as Los Angles in the Southwest, Miami in the Southeast, Alaska in the Northwest, and as far as New Hampshire in the Northeast. Visited the Atlantic and Pacific Oceans.

If I haven't bored you to sleep with the previous stuff, I just want to mention that as a reenactor, in addition to the 6 seasons as a professional Santa, I have appeared as mounted militia man in the Guardian of the Kentucky Road documentary (William Whitley) and a long hunter in The Wilderness Road at Martin's Station film.

Chapter 8
Dispatching Goliath from Our Government

I don't know if I can claim expertise in anything. It's true that I have done a lot of different things in my eighty years (both personally & professionally) and I have diligently sought to do those things with excellence. The Lord has blessed me with so many opportunities, and I am humbled by His favor. One area where I possess no expert wisdom is politics. Of all the agendas I have pursued throughout my life, politics was not one I planned to complete. Most of us will agree that there are things left to be desired at the national, state, and local levels. While it is certainly easy for me to criticize what I don't like, I am hesitant to do so. I am not in those folks' shoes/positions. I know, some things seem obvious. When it comes to party politics — well, let's face it, we often think the other side is wrong and our side is right. Not much surprises me on the political front. I look at current events and happenings against the backdrop of Scripture. This is especially true for me relative to the doctrine of eschatology/last things/last days. So, I don't get overly excited. Although it may not seem like it, God is in control of the universe and that just happens to include our tiny planet called earth. Goliath thinks he is in charge. Oh, undoubtedly, he is running roughshod but not really in control of the big picture, the eternal promises. Of course, the thing that exacerbates our negative view of what's going on in the world and especially our country is when we feel the pinch. When groceries, fuel, rent, new homes, vehicles, utilities, health care, taxes. etc. hover over us at all-time highs we are not happy campers, nor should we be expected to be delighted. English writer and philosopher, Aldous Huxley, said, "Experience is not what happens to a man; it is what a man does with what happens to him." Where our freedom often seems controlled by political forces, I guess we are "caught in a trap" (as Elvis might say) of doing the best we can with what we have. Sure, it isn't something we would call satisfaction. While Huxley's work Brave New World is not something

I would guide my life by, wouldn't it be wonderful to have a world that gets it right.

Let me hasten to do a disclaimer, I love people of all political parties, the primary parties being Democrat, Republican, and Independent. It's always my hope or at least wish that we can all agree to disagree. I may not be able to agree with or endorse the political views of a person, when those views are at cross purposes with mine. However, the Bible teaches us to "love one another." I have no problem praying for those who would choose to be my enemies, persecute me, or despitefully use me. I won't agree with certain positions, and I will be cautious.

As far back as I can remember, my ancestors right down through my grandparents and parents were Democrats. That's how I grew up. As most people do, I followed that path. Several years ago, Carol and I changed parties and became registered Republicans. The main reason is that the other party seemed to be moving more away from our core values, principles, and beliefs. Carol's background was similar, although her dad was a Democrat and her mom a Republican. The secondary reason for changing parties is because of us living in a Republican county. There were too many candidates for whom we could not cast a vote. I don't question that there are Democrats who are more conservative.

Realizing that Republicans aren't perfect, I still feel more comfortable with the conservative platform the party represents. I have been a loyal member of my party just as I was when I was a registered voter in the other party. Incidentally, my best friend is an Independent. I am not trying to be "Mr. Republican" but I am an active supporter and participant. As alluded to in an earlier chapter, in 2023, my party honored me by inducting me into the Republican 5th District Lincoln Club Hall of Fame. I was very humbled to be selected with two other people from the 30 counties of the district, with a Republican voting base of nearly 311,000. Congressman Harold Rogers has been a tremendous asset in our district and he has always had my support. His garnering funds for our needs when I was with the city was extremely helpful. He has been a real friend to Mt. Vernon and Rockcastle County. He is one who gets it, in that he "represents" his district.

Kentucky's two Kentucky US Senators are Republican. They are Senator Mitch McConnell and Senator Rand Paul. They too, like Congressman Rogers, are friends of mine and I have worked with them. We have five Republican Kentucky US Representatives and one Democrat Kentucky US Representative. Our Kentucky Governor and Lieutenant Governor are Democrat.

Every day I pray for our state and our nation, as well as our local community. My prayer is that all our leaders will know and follow the Lord. I said earlier that I don't consider myself an expert on politics. However, my twelve years in office taught me a great deal.

Although reluctant to file for office (I sort of got drafted), in 2010 I filed as a candidate for Mayor of the City of Mt. Vernon. After a seven-month campaign, I was elected. I had two opponents. Four years later I faced two different candidates, then into my second campaign. I won by a better margin than in the first race. Four years after that I faced just one competitor in my third bid for office. I won by an even better margin. When I ran the first time, I was 65 and retired. You can see why I kind of went kicking and screaming at the idea of running.

Unfortunately, when I ran the first time it was quite stressful. It wasn't just because politics was a new endeavor for me but because City Hall was sitting under a dark cloud. Some legal problems occurred with the previous administration that ended in a resignation by the mayor. The interim mayor who was in office for a few months before I assumed office helped to lift that cloud some. However, fully restoring the character and image of the city would require a longer time. So, of course I saw that as my first mandate. After a few months we were able to accomplish that goal. In fact, not having a mayoral record on which to run, my first campaign was primarily running on my own character. At the same time, I had a platform that included no promises but goals for the city. During the time I was Mayor, my oldest son, Michael, ran for State Representative (in 3 counties) and later for State Senate (in 6 counties). Our youngest son, Matt, ran a county race for PVA. It is interesting that a family who had no ambition relative to politics ended up running 6 races. It was exhausting. We all helped one another. Sons Michael and Matt co-chaired all three of my campaigns. The mayoral position is nonpartisan. I enjoyed the support of Republicans, Democrats, and Independents. Crucial to my campaign efforts were some Democrats and Independents.

Carol and I loved Rockcastle County and Mt. Vernon, having spent a total of 50 years here before her passing. Now, I have been here two and a half years beyond that. Mt. Vernon is a small, close-knit community nestled in some small hills and in a county of 300 square miles. Seventy percent of our county is wooded, with a portion of that being Daniel Boone National Forest. Between Lake Linville, farm ponds, creeks and streams of all kinds, and a nationally recognized wild river called the Rockcastle, it is a great place for fishing. Whether you are a bass fisherman or a pan fisherman, there are angling opportunities for everyone. Some great deer, turkey, and small game hunting here. Hiking and horseback trails galore. Even have a place called Little Egypt. We have one of the top respirator patient hospitals in the nation, along with other health care services. Our public school system is matchless. Mt. Vernon is the county seat. Livingston is located just south of us and is designated as a State Trail Town. Brodhead to our west has its own unique and colorful offerings — including the location of the county fair. There is an active industrial authority and development board. My friend Jeff Vanhook has helped to open doors of opportunity for us to grow and eventually employ several people. While no community is perfect, in my opinion this is a great place to raise a family or retire. Carol and I did both. We have some industry, several businesses (at the time I left office, the city was selling almost a hundred business licenses per year for those located here and those coming here to do business), a railroad spur, two I-75 Interstate exits and a short drive to Berea, Richmond, Lexington, London, Corbin, and Somerset, a Chamber of Commerce (which Carol and I were both made lifetime honorary members of when I decided not to run again for office). Other attractions are Renfro Valley Entertainment Center and the Kentucky Music Hall of Fame.

We have also had state senators and state representatives from our county, as well as state appellate judges and state supreme court justices. At least two have become state chief justice of the supreme court.

Although Mt. Vernon is a small city, there are 7 departments (counting the complex at Lake Linville), around 35 employees, and a multimillion dollar budget. I was delighted to leave office with twelve clean audits. The lake is the city's water source. The city owns around 276 acres of lake, the perimeter of the lake, the bait shop, the docks, the campground, and leases a dwelling that houses a great restaurant. Around 400 acres are owned in total. Also, the lake property has a park, picnic ground, splash pad, and a Veteran's Park. In addition to having around two thousand homes and businesses as retail customers, the city wholesales water to fringe areas of about 5 counties. The city's first responders, police and fire & rescue are well trained and well equipped. There is also a sheriff's department, and a certain number of state troopers assigned here, along with some constables. The Mt. Vernon Police Department has Chief Joe Rush,

Assistant Brian Carter, along with several other officers. The schools are protected by officers with the MVPD through a contract with the Rockcastle County School System. School Superintendent Dr. Carrie Ballinger does a super job in leading our educational system. I am also grateful for friends, Sheriff Shannon Franklin (and former Sheriffs Darrel Doan and the late Sheriffs William Taylor and Shirley Smith, my retired State Trooper buddies the late Jimmy Silvers, Jack Lawless, Gary Lane, John Yates, Darren Allen, and my Trooper friends Lafe Owens and Ben Allen. County Judge Executive Howell Holbrook, the magistrates, County Court Clerk Danetta Allen, Circuit Court Clerk Eliza York, PVA Janet Vaughn, County Attorney Jeremy Rowe, Assistant County Attorney William Leger, Jailer Nathan Carter and all our other county officials are appreciated and among my friends. I had also worked with my friends Buzz Carloftis and Doug Bishop, who were County Judge Executives. When I was in office it was a pleasure working with my friends, Mayor Jason Medley of Livingston and Mayor Walter Cash of Brodhead. The City of Mt. Vernon's city government is composed of a six member council (legislative branch) and mayor (executive branch). State Supreme Court Justice Debbie Lambert, State Appellate Judge James Lambert,

Travis Burton (State Chamber of Commerce), State Agriculture Commissioner Jonathan Shell, John Hughes (Representative for State Representative Andy Barr), Assistant Solicitor General Grant Burdette at Kentucky Attorney General's Office & Rockcastle County Republican Party Chairman, and city Attorney Bobby Amburgy are all friends. Tim Roberts succeeded me as mayor and is still in office as of this writing.

Having served 12 years in the mayor's office, I am the second longest serving Mayor in the city's history. I served 12 years and former Mayor Roland Mullins served 14. When I was in office, we constructed a Wall of Mayors in the City Council chambers. This display contains photographs and years served.

I am proud to report that during my tenure we made significant strides in every department. My hat is off to the department heads I had at that time, as well as the administrative staff. The admin folks are the same as when I was there. They were great to work with and became my work family. Jill Medley is the Water Clerk, Crystal Rush is the City Clerk, Becky Payne is the Tax Administrator, and Nicole Roberts is the receptionist. Jill, Crystal, and Nicole all served at one time or another as my assistant. Josh Bray was with the city for several years.

He served as the Tax Commissioner and City Administrator. State Representative Bray, who has a degree in accounting, was my left and right hands regarding the budget and other financial matters. While I think he may still do some contract work with the city, for the past several years he has been our State Representative. Louise Kirby was our janitor during the 12 years I was in office (and before that). No one could have asked for a sweeter person or someone who kept everything spic and span for us. She promised to stay with me as long as I was in office, and she did. When she learned I was not running again, she retired shortly before I left.

If only being the mayor would mean just cutting ribbons and kissing babies, it would be great. Nope! I had more than my share of challenges and headaches. While in office, I was sued 4 times. I won every lawsuit, including one that went all the way to the State Supreme Court. I am glad to no longer be in the political arena but thankful that I could serve our wonderful people in that capacity. We did not get everything done (that never happens) but together we moved our town forward and made it at least a little better place to live. Speaking of which, I want to give honorable mention to my good friend Lynn Tatum. Lynn is the Executive Director of the Rockcastle County Development

Board and very active in the Chamber, and she serves on the Kentucky Music Hall of Fame Museum & Tourism board. Lynn was the first person I hired when I went to work for the city. We named her our Vitalize Mt. Vernon Director. For years now, she has worked tirelessly to improve and beautify our town. She has done a great job! Neal Sluder, owner of the Lone Star farm store and friend, was the chairman of the KMHOF during the last years of my tenure. Friend Roy Martin had also served in that capacity. The twelve years I spent in office left me feeling both honored and humbled. I enjoyed the overwhelming support of the town. For that I will always be grateful. Carol and I made so many friends in our wonderful town.

Our world, our nation, our state, our communities are ravaged with crime, violence, and addictions. Speaking of addictions, thankfully I have never smoked marijuana or used other drugs. I drank alcohol while I was in high school. After graduating high school, alcohol had no appeal to me. I guess it was more of a peer thing. My friends drank and so did I. Also, I was quite young when I entered the ministry. Even before that, I stopped drinking. When I was in high school drinking for me only occurred infrequently. It was mainly those times when I was "partying." I never got hooked on it. I am aware that there are different schools of thought relative to drinking alcohol. People have to make their own choices about it. The Bible is very clear about drunkenness. It's message is don't. I choose not to drink alcohol at all. Just think if I had continued with it over all these years. Being a teetotaler, I still got diagnosed with cirrhosis of the liver at age 77. Alcohol would have likely killed me way before now. I know there are those who drink socially. Apparently, some folks can handle that and don't get drunk or become alcoholics. Another problem with alcohol is that it is notorious for killing brain cells that do not regenerate. Others, who may have a greater propensity to alcoholism find out when it is too late. Frankly, I prefer to take my last breath and leave this world without the smell of alcohol on my breath. I remember responding to a vehicle accident one night when I was with the sheriff's department, where one of the occupants was ejected from the vehicle. Before dying, the young man in his twenties lay there in the road screaming God's name in vain. He was drunk. Each of us will answer for all the things we have done in this life and those things that we failed to do. With my years of ministry, counseling, ambulance work, social work, and law enforcement, I have seen more than my share of the devastation caused by drugs and alcohol. If there is anyway Goliath can get his foot in the door to use these things to violate God's will for us, he will do it.

Goliath pulls out all the stops to attack and damage our government at all levels. That's why it is imperative that we have God-fearing people leading us. The Bible says in the Apostle Paul's teaching about government leaders, "...pay ye tribute also: for they are God's ministers, attending continually upon this very thing. Render therefore to all their dues: tribute to whom tribute is due; custom to whom is custom; fear to whom fear; honour to whom honour." (Romans 13:6-7). The New International Version (NIV) reads this way, "This is also why you pay taxes, for the authorities are God's servants, who give their full time to governing. Give to everyone what you owe them: If you owe taxes, pay taxes; if revenue, then revenue; if respect, then respect; if honor, then honor." Then, there is 1 Peter 2:13-14 in the NIV, "Submit yourself for the Lord's sake to every human authority, or to governors who are sent by him to punish those who do wrong and to commend those who do right." 1 Timothy 2:1-2 admonishes us to pray and give thanks for everyone, including kings and all those in positions of authority. Paul, writing to Timothy, also makes the point that by doing this it helps us to lead a quiet and peaceable life.

Obviously, if it violates the teachings of the Bible or goes against God's will—well, that's another matter. I personally see my mantra as "God first, family second, the body of Christ third (church), then friends, government, etc." It has been my motto for years that I am not necessarily against everything that is politically correct, providing it does not infringe upon that which is spiritually and biblically correct.

To me, God must be active in the affairs of mankind (humankind) for us to have true peace and harmony. One thing you can bank on, Goliath has no place. Goliath is to be dispatched forthwith from government. Pray for our leaders! Pray that God will send Christian leaders to fill the halls of government at the local, state, and national levels. Our ultimate hierarchy is the Lord. Years ago, Watchman Nee wrote a book on Spiritual Authority. The bottom line, and where "the rubber meets the road" is, at all times God is our ultimate authority. Anything and anyone who messes with that is out of line. The best decisions are always those that are guided by the Holy Spirit. Try to substitute anything else and we are asking Goliath to take the wheel—that's an accident waiting to happen that spells disaster.

Chapter 9
Dispatching Goliath from Our Health

Exodus 15:26, God says to His people, "...I am the Lord that healeth thee." The name of the Lord in this verse is Rapha, which is one of His many names. The meaning here is "the Lord our Healer!" There are a number of biblical references about healing. I do want to say right up front that God heals every born-again believer spiritually the moment of accepting Jesus as Savior. Sometimes He does physical healing while we are on earth, but He *always* heals after death. It is tragic that some in the name of ministry have made a travesty of "performing" healings. I don't question God's power. I don't doubt the anointing or that people are healed. It may take place in the privacy and quietness of one's home, in a church service, or wherever. The Bible makes it clear that nothing is impossible for our God. I believe in miracles. Sometimes the Lord will merely speak it and call it done. Sometimes He may do it over time. Sometimes He may choose to use medical personnel and/or medications—even the holistic, natural herbs He planted here in the earth's first pharmacy. I will not dare judge anyone who claims to be a faith healer. I am open to whatever the Holy Spirit chooses to do. I will only say that in my discernment sometimes I struggle within my spirit bearing witness with certain faith healers. God loves us, cares for us, provides for us. Those of us who know Jesus are His children. The Lord is so giving, so generous. However, what I struggle with is ministers who become multimillionaires from ministry, those who live lavish lifestyles at the expense of the poor widow's donation, who barely survives. As investigative reporters discover behind the scenes activities of some of these ministry organizations, their findings are often disillusioning and disappointing. The Bible warns us about false prophets. Do I believe in divine healing? Absolutely! I have observed it occurring among family, friends, and former church members. Never, ever limit our God who is omniscient, omnipotent, and omnipresent. When I underwent coronary bypass in 2005 my heart surgeon told me that I had ten more years, if I took really good care of myself. It has now been twenty years. When Carol had the massive stroke doctors told us nothing could be done, and that we needed to pray. She lived for six more years. How did we survive longer? It is what God does!

Some quickly criticize and deride those who lay hands on folks and anoint them with oil. Careful! There is a Scriptural basis and teaching for such ministerial actions. I am willing to pray for anyone anywhere for healing. Let us not quench or grieve the Holy Spirit.

I heard Dr. Leo Eddelman, former President of the New Orleans Baptist Theological Seminary, speak many years ago. On that occasion he mentioned having a daughter who was a physician. He said that someone asked her if she believed in divine healing. She responded with this question, "Is there any other kind?"

During my 60 years of ministering I have stood at the bedside of those who were dying (including my own mother and my dear wife Carol). I never hesitate to pray for people to be healed, no matter how sick they are. We believe in a Lord that cleansed leprosy, made the lame to walk, the blind to see, and bring back the dead from the grave. Does

God's will have anything to do with it? Of course, it has everything to do with it. God has a divine will and a permissive will. He bids us to do His divine will. He also allows us to operate outside of His will but remember robots can't love you. We refer to it as free, moral choice. Asking according to His will is what He wants. Why would I trust my will over His? Who is always right? God or me?

Carol and I both experienced a reprieve from an earlier death. She is gone and I am still here but we both experienced miraculous extensions. Keep in mind that no matter what happens to us here on earth (whether we are healed or not) God heals every believer who goes to Heaven, never to experience sickness again.

Watching our loved ones and friends suffer is difficult. Being without them is difficult. At the age I am now, I have lost grandparents, parents, my sister, a nephew, almost 30 aunts and uncles, several first and second cousins, and countless friends and acquaintances. Of course, losing my soulmate is the most difficult of all. Believe me when I tell you that I understand poor health, illness, sickness, as well as death. I was exposed to a few deaths as a boy and as a teenager. During the past 60 years it has been heavy — the loss of family and friends, conducting numerous funerals, and working for three funeral homes. Then, of course there is law enforcement. I have seen my share of carnage with accidents, homicides, suicides. I don't know what is ahead, except I know I have now lived most of my years and I have threatening illnesses (some life threatening). I am now on the other end of the spectrum. I leave it with the Lord. That gives me peace. I want to go when He is ready for me. There is so much to look forward to in Heaven. In the meantime, as much as I am able, I will continue living on my own, taking care of my cabin, attending church, visiting the cemetery, visiting with family, cooking & baking, running errands, going to an incredible amount of medical appointments, shopping, attending auctions and rodeos, reading, watching the old westerns and other types of reruns, supporting my sports teams, listening to praise & worship music, doing daily devotions, listening to 50's, 60's, 70's music, and whatever the Lord wants me to do. While I am limited in traveling long distances, I can drive reasonable distances, reenact, maybe do some fishing and hunting now and then. God is good!

At the risk of boring you with my health status, I want to share some things I face these days. My purpose is to give God all praise and glory for sustaining me as He has. Also, I am hoping to encourage those of you who are going through some tough times of your own.

After being at Carol's side during 2007-2008 while she battled two kinds of cancer that necessitated surgery, chemo, and radiation—and with her in 2015 when she had numerous mini strokes and seizures, and finally a major stroke—then in 2017 when her massive stroke occurred, leaving her confined in a wheelchair until she passed in 2023, the hospitalizations, doctor appointments, procedures, therapy, etc.—well, we were older and not physically able to do what we once did. Nonetheless, we kept going and refused to forfeit our quality of life. Of course, those last 6 years I was her primary caregiver but was still in public office and had major back surgery. Some of our days were spent staying in the same room in the rehab facility with both of us recovering and receiving therapy. Several years before, we cared for elderly and infirmed parents. I promised her while she was in the medical facilities for three months that upon coming home, we would still live our lives, and we did!

As a child I had some of the usual childhood maladies, such as chicken pox, flu, a broken arm, tonsils and adenoids removed, a serious sledding accident, and so forth. At the end of my 8th grade year, I contracted mono. When I was a freshman in high school, I had an appendectomy and developed pneumonia, while I still had mono. I spent two weeks in the hospital. I stayed reasonably healthy (except for flu, etc.), until I underwent open heart surgery in 2005. My 4 bypasses included blockages of one 70%, two 90%, and one 100%, including the aorta. I've had 12 different surgeries, including major back surgery after Carol was in the wheelchair. One month to the day of Carol leaving for her Heavenly homegoing, I was diagnosed with stage 3 cirrhosis of the liver (I am a non-alcohol drinker). I had internal bleeding in my esophagus. They gave me two units of blood and flew me by helicopter to Lexington. Surgery was done, and then another one later for the same thing. Stage 3 cirrhosis includes esophageal variceal bleeding, ascites (abdominal fluid buildup), neuropathy and sometimes gout, and many other symptoms, all triggered by the cirrhosis. I've had 14 skin biopsies. Thankfully, they all came back benign except for one on my upper right arm. It was melanoma and required surgery but now I am fine, so far. The lower lobe of my right lung collapsed. My pulmonologist doesn't know how it happened and there is nothing they can do to fix it. My breathing is normal, unless I exert myself very much. There are more "gory" details, but I will spare you. I will only say that daily I battle things such as nausea, other digestive issues, pain, weakness, and over all just not feeling well. Even with problems with my eyes, it is possible that too is a result of the cirrhosis. During my lifetime I have been an in-patient in three states and 8 hospitals. I also made ER visits in yet another state. Yes, it is tempting with my grief and illness to say I have a "Job complex" but not really. I would never compare my suffering to that of Job. With my indescribable grief, and all that I have gone through and am going through, I am not angry and I don't feel cheated. God gave me lots of years of good health and lots of years with my sweetheart. I miss her terribly but look forward to being reunited with her. I have learned in my life's pilgrimage that life does not furnish us with a wishing wand or a genie in a bottle. No magic bullets are available. Because of the original sin, at birth we begin our journey toward our final destination — death!

I run myself ragged picking up prescriptions and getting to all my medical appointments, as well as having medical tests regularly. I currently am under the care of my primary, gastroenterologist, pulmonologist, dermatologist, cardiologist, nephrologist, optometrist, chiropractor, physical therapist, and dentist. I guess you could say I am non-discriminatory *LOL*. I should feel important with such a huge bunch of medical personnel, but it is more like dependent. I would like to mention my medical team by name. I am receiving excellent health care from them. I need them now more than ever before. Over the years I have been given good medical cared by others. Going back to when I was a boy I remember primary caregivers. They were once called just doctor, general practitioner, family care physician. My primary physicians whose names I remember were Claxton, Phelan, Helzerman, Blanton, Bunch, Prewitt, Catron, Lewis, Arvin, Griffith, and Bullock. Currently the following are my health care providers.

- Dr. Benjamin Taylor, Primary, Baptist Health, Berea
- Dr. Jagannath Sherigar, Gastroenterologist, Baptist Health, Richmond
- PA Sara Chasteen, Gastroenterology, Baptist Health, Richmond
- Dr. Larry Todd Breeding, Cardiologist, Baptist Health, Richmond
- Dr. Caleb Meenach, Pulmonologist, Baptist Health, Lexington
- Dr. John Roth, Dermatologist, Lexington
- Muhammad Farhan, Nephrologist, Nephrology Associates of Kentuckiana, Richmond

(affiliated with Baptist Health)

- Dr. Kevin Skidmore, Optometrist, King's Eye Care, Berea
- Dr. Wade Davis, Chiropractor, Davis Chiropractic, Mt. Vernon
- Dr. Lura Cash, Dentist, Rockcastle Family Dental Center, Rockcastle Regional, Mt. Vernon
- Physical Therapists, Rockcastle Regional, Mt. Vernon

At the age I am now, it takes an "army" of folks to keep me propped up. I am very grateful to all of those who have treated me during the past eighty years. At this time, I have a tremendous team of professional and caring health care providers. I see my specialists at certain times, depending on what is prescribed for my conditions. My primary, along with most of my specialists, are in the Baptist Health network. Dr. Benjamin Taylor, as my primary, sees me frequently and coordinates my overall health care with the other folks I see. Not only is Dr. Taylor a competent physician but is extremely patient and caring. His staff is also outstanding. I am treated like family. Many thanks to Medical Assistant Whitney Kunce, Receptionist Kaetlyn Ballard, and Lab Technician Annette Disque. All the folks on board there are friendly and compassionate.

Another word about Dr. Taylor is that he goes beyond what is expected from a primary. His attention to detail, treatment, and follow-up are nothing short of excellent. He has the heavy lifting because of coordinating my care with several specialists.

I promise you that I am not listing my ailments to elicit sympathy. With all that's happening and is still happening in my life, my faith in the Lord is stronger than it has ever been. I never have to search for God. He is right here with me. I hope that someone can find inspiration and strength from what I am sharing. I want to be healed. I want to be healthy. I never envisioned my last days being like this. It is okay. Staying or leaving, I win! I know how it all ends — or should I say begins. We stay on earth for a few years and then the best is yet to come, if we have Jesus in our heart! The alternative? Well, that is a more precipitous direction than we want to even think about. Yes, I believe the Bible. I believe Heaven is sweet and Hell is hot!!!!!" There is a town in Michigan named Hell. The small, incorporated town became an official entity in 1841. It is probably less than fifty miles from where I grew up. However, I never went there, and I don't want to go to the one prepared for the devil and his angels.

There is also a small community in Eastern Kentucky (Leslie County) named Hell for Certain. The good news? No one needs to go there. It is only by choice. Choose Jesus and you choose Heaven.

When they were preparing me for my heart valve replacement procedure the anesthesiologist spoke with me. He told me I would have four doctors in the OR. When they wheeled me into the OR I looked around. I saw this same doctor. I said to him, "I see we have 5 doctors." He replied, "No, remember I told you 4." I continued to insist that there were 5. He asks, "Are you a doctor?" I said, "Yes but not the kind that makes money." Then, I pointed up toward the ceiling and said to him, "I mean my Chief of Staff, the Great Physician." God, my healer is always in charge of my health! We may not know what is next, pertaining to our health, but one thing I do know — if we know the Lord, He never leaves us or forsakes us, He never stops loving us and caring for us.

Chapter 10
Goliath Needs to Be Dispatched from the Word & Prayer

The Word

The Bible has been around for a longtime. Haven't we read it enough? Many of us grew up with the Word of God. We pretty much know what it says. We are aware of the message. Besides, it was written centuries ago. How relevant can it be now? As Dr. Billy Graham used to say, "It is as current as today's newspaper." I began preaching 60 years ago. I have served in various ministry capacities, I have studied, pursued formal training, I have preached and taught the Word, why do I need to spend daily devotional time that includes the Bible? It is simple. It is the true, inerrant, infallible, living

Word of God. It never gets old. I am still learning from it. It is not just another book—it is the BOOK of books. It has been and continues to be the world's best seller. It is unique in several ways. One is the fact that it is a composite of 66 books (39 in the Old Testament and 27 in the New Testament) within one book. It has been said that every answer we need in life is in that book. I agree. I have found that to be so true. It is my roadmap, my compass, and my GPS. I cannot imagine life without its comfort and guidance. John 1:1, says, "In the beginning was the Word, and the Word was with God, and the Word was God." The reference here is not the Word as such, the Bible. The Bible was still being written. Jesus is that living Word. The coming of Jesus as the Messiah was prophesied in the Old Testament and fulfilled with His birth in Bethlehem, as recorded in the Bible in the New Testament. His footprints are all over the pages of the books of the New Testament. He was the Word incarnate. Are you struggling to believe the Bible? Well, look around you. Prophecy from the Old Testament is being fulfilled right now at an unprecedented rate. In the New Testament (especially the Book of Revelation) the words relative to the last days are rapidly moving to a close. Archaeology continues to confirm the truth of Scripture. I am excited and overjoyed with what Jesus has promised to His true church, true believers who have placed their trust and their lives in Him.

Please don't stumble through life without the Word, both the Bible and Jesus. I love folks. I would not ask anyone to do something I haven't done. I promise you that as the hymn says, "there's no other way to be happy in Jesus, but to trust and obey." The hymn, "Trust and Obey," was written by John H. Sammis, a Presbyterian minister. It was published in 1887. There has been no better way before Sammis published the hymn and no better way ever since. Are we to obey our earthly mother and father? Should we do any less for our Heavenly Father? He is our Creator, our Life Giver. Isn't the Bible just for the ignorant and uneducated? Some "intelligent" people (or are they?) may think that. Very interesting, when we have recently become aware of the person known to have the highest IQ is a man by the name of Dr. YoungHoon Kim (IQ of 276) who recently said, "I believe that Jesus Christ is God, the way and the truth and the life."

Can you imagine what it would be like without the Bible? We would not know where we came from. We would not know about the future and what God has planned. We would not have the guidance and direction that helps us to live happy

and fulfilled lives. We would not know how to receive our wonderful Savior and would not know
that by accepting Him we have eternal life. We
would know nothing of the Holy Spirit, the one
who convicts, comforts, and fills us. The Bible has
something for everyone — history, science, poetry,
understanding of right and wrong, Christian living.
It has lyrics set to music, miracles, marriage, family
life, God's promises, and the list goes on. Fulfill-
ment of prophecy, those archaeological discoveries,
His Spirit bearing witness with our spirit are all
confirmation of its veracity. Yes, our world is not all
it should be. Just think of our not being taught at an
early age to not lie, not steal, not covet, not be un-
faithful to our marriage vows, not murder, and
know that our bodies are to be temples of the Holy
Spriit. The Word teaches us about love, grace,
mercy, forgiveness, relationships, and much more.
How do we know we came from dirt (dust) and
that's where these earthly shells, houses, bodies will
finish? Why do we busy ourselves with material-
ism? Who told us we will be here forever? Not so.
Paul tells us that "if in this life only we have hope
in Christ, we are of all men most miserable." 1 Corinthians 15:19

By reading the Bible we learn that the Scripture
is this, "All scripture is given by inspiration of God,

and is profitable for doctrine, for reproof, for correction, for instruction in righteousness." The song written for children "The B-I-B-L-E That's the Book for Me" says:

> The B-I-B-L-E yes, that's the book for me. I stand alone on the Word of God the Bible.

The BIBLE, yes, that's the book for me. I love to hear the stories from the BIBLE.

The BIBLE, yes, that's the book for me. I'll read and study the Word of God the BIBLE

Never take for granted this special jewel the Lord has provided—the Bible, God's Word! Hebrews 4:12 says, "For the Word of God is quick, and powerful, and sharper than any two-edged sword, piercing even to the dividing asunder of soul and spirit, and of the joints and marrow, and is a discerner of the thoughts, and intents of the heart."

Isaiah 55:11, "So shall my word be that goeth out of my mouth: it shall not return unto me void, but it shall accomplish that which I please, and it shall prosper in the thing whereunto I sent it."

Proverbs 30:5, "Every word of God is pure..."

Matthew 24:35 Jesus said, "Heaven and earth shall pass away but my words shall not pass away."

Isaiah 40:8, "The grass withereth , the flower fadeth: but the word of our God shall stand forever." Everything in life is transient except the Word of God.

Psalm 119:89, "Forever, O Lord, thy word is settled in heaven."

Psalm 119:130, "The entrance of thy words giveth light; it giveth understanding unto the simple."

In Ephesians 6:17 Paul stated that part of the armor for the Chrisitan is to be "the sword of the Spirit, which is the Word of God." Obviously then, we should wear that armor at all times.

In Luke 11:28 Jesus taught, "...blessed are they that hear the word of God and keep it."

The verses I shared above about God's precious words are just some of many. There is no substitute for His Word. For many years translations other than the King James Version have been published. It is true the KJV was released in 1611 by the English King James. It does seem to have been a political maneuver on the King's part. It was favorable for him to have the Bible printed in the language of his people (The Old English) and shore up his being the head of the Church of England. That's why some of the language is different than the way we talk today with our modern English. Whatever King James' motive, it was a good move to have the translators go back to the original manuscripts for translation. That makes the version accurate and trustworthy. In the many years since 1611, among all the different translations, we now have accuracy with at least some of them. A word of caution is everything that has been published may not necessarily consistently and accurately match the Hebrew and Greek original text of God's Word. Do your research before relying on something that may or may not be that accurate. Also, be tuned into things such as paraphrases. They may be good for easy reading and understanding. However, if you are interested in a serious study of the Word, they may lack what you need. Over the course of many years now I have read and studied from other translations that I think are dependable. The reason I chose to use the KJV for this writing is because it is a beautiful translation, I grew up on it, and because in the region where I live it is the one most often read and carried. It's also why I use it in the pulpit. Admittedly, I have found it necessary at times to interpret the Old English before I could get to the message of the text.

Bottom line about the Holy Bible is to daily read and study it. You will never learn it all. It equips and strengthens us. Daily Bible reading, prayer, and worship all need to be a significant activity in the believer's life. It's not how much time you spend each day but make it quality time with the Lord. D.L. Moody said, "It's not enough to simply possess the Spirit; the Spirit must possess you." As the Bible tells us to "not forsake the assembling of ourselves together" (be involved in a Bible believing church), carry your Bible to church with you. Don't let it stop there. Look at the Word each day. None of us is strong enough without the meat of His Holy Word!

Yes, our enemy Goliath (that ole' serpent) wants us to ignore the reading and study of the Word of God. It reveals that he is that liar and the father of lies. Reading our Bibles makes him cringe. It threatens him and his platform, his mission to "steal, kill, and destroy." It doesn't matter what he wants. He only gets to win if we let him. Just don't ignore the Word. Don't fail to see it as a daily necessity for our lives. Don't refuse to carry this weapon that overcomes the enemy. It's our armament. Don't take a vacation from it, even when you are "on vacation." If we are remiss in making the Word a practice in our lives, it helps Goliath to fortify his own weaponry. Don't let him win. Dispatch that sinister dude.

Prayer

Recently I purchased a small sign to display in

my cabin. It says, "Pray Big. Worry Small." One I saw years ago said, "Why worry when you can pray." I am afraid that all too often even believers reverse these. Goliath wants us to engage in worry, God wants us to pray. Do you think if worry knocked on the door and prayer answered, that suddenly worry would be gone? Yes, it most likely will leave. Then, why do we insist sometimes on choosing to worry. Of course, there are many things in life that clamor for our attention. We can go through some turbulent waters. I won't pretend that as Christians we don't face plenty of negativity in our journey. Sometimes it may originate with other people, sometimes because of circumstances and maybe even because we listened to the enemy. In no way am I suggesting that we are not going to be concerned about many different things in life. As I think of my own physical maladies, of course I am concerned. However, I try to live my life as best I can, go to sleep at night and leave the rest to the Lord. He did not promise there would be no turbulent waters but He promised to stay with us through it all.

In Matthew 6:9-13 Jesus gives us a guide, sort of an outline for prayer. I think there was no expectation on the Savior's part for His disciples or others to necessarily pray verbatim the prayer. He was careful to include things in the prayer that were important. Jesus disseminated the information during His renown Sermon on the Mount. The model He gave then is still excellent for today. On another occasion Jesus provided a similar model in Luke 11. Following is the prayer in Matthew's gospel.

Model Prayer
Matthew 6:9-13

After this manner therefore pray ye: Our Father which art in heaven, Hallowed be thy name.

Thy kingdom come. Thy will be done in earth, as it is in heaven.

Give us this day our daily bread.

And forgive us our debts, as we forgive our debtors.

And lead us not into temptation, but deliver us from evil: For thine is the is the kingdom, and the power, and the glory, forever. Amen

For the most part, I am not going to dissect the prayer here. I have taught and preached it. Many scholars have written books about it with a detailed treatise of the subject. Beautiful songs have been

Chapter 11
Dispatching Goliath from Our Confidence/Faith for the Last Days

A study of the "Last Days" (doctrine of eschatology) is important. It is not something to be ignored, even if you have difficulty understanding all the details. God has provided it in His Word for our benefit. Granted, it is not the easiest among the Scriptures to grasp. However, the information is full of "gold nuggets" and it pertains to every person who has been born. Numerous books have been written about the subject, authors with more expertise than I have. I appreciate those scholars who have given us the advantage of their interpretation of such significant passages. There are videos, podcasts, lectures on understanding this most pertinent topic.

Right up front I am doing a disclaimer here, I am not an expert on the end times. I am thankful to have had the opportunity to study, teach, and preach about these futuristic events. It's exciting. Perhaps my rendering here is unnecessary. In praying about what the Lord wanted me to include in this writing, this is part of the content I think He wanted included here. It is timely.

In an earlier chapter I alluded to some things about the wrap up but now I want to elaborate. As I said in my previous chapter, at best some of what I share will be controversial among those who have a different view. That's okay. I respect differing views. This is simply my interpretation based on my study. In 2 Peter 1:20 Peter tells his readers, "…no prophecy of the scripture is of any private interpretation."

In the Old Testament we have the prophecy of occurrences in the last days. This includes some from Jeremiah and Ezekiel, with the primary sources being Isaiah, Daniel, Zechariah, and Joel. As one reads those Old Testament passages, the link to the New Testament is clear. Compared to those scholarly minds who go into great depth, my information may seem elementary. However, I hope you as the reader will find it helpful. Keep in mind that the Book of Revelation is to be approached with an understanding that it involves past, present, future, as well as signs, symbols, etc.

First, we need to identify the Church Age, time period in which we are now living. This period began when the Holy Spirit came, as recorded in the Book of Acts. This was at Pentecost. This era will last until the Rapture of the church, the body of Christ. During an earlier period of this church age the Lord challenges and pleads with the seven churches of Asia Minor (today's Turkey). The seven churches identified in the Book of Revelation are Ephesus, Smyrna, Pergamum, Thyatira. Sardis, Philadelphia, and Laodicea. What was the status of these churches in the Roman province when the Lord addressed them. Let's break it down. These messages were delivered to the Apostle John in a revelation from Jesus. God gave it to Jesus and then Jesus to John while John was on the Island of Patmos, where he had been exiled because of his faith. Oftentimes, what Goliath (the enemy) intends for bad God turns into good. Something else that is notable is when John received the revelation he was in the Spirit and it was on the Lord's Day. Isn't it wonderful how the Lord uses us. Some may perceive that the group of disciples that followed Jesus, His close friends that ministered with Him, were misfits. Some examples are a tax collector (much hated by many), hot headedness, uneducated, etc. It is still often the case. When the Lord called me to preach, I didn't feel fit, worthy, or capable. I still feel that way. At a church I pastored some years ago a gentleman in our church said to me one day, "Pastor Mike, you've got a bunch of misfits here." I replied with a question, "Aren't we all misfits?"

Now, let's look at the Ephesus church (Revelation 2:1-7). What was the problem? According to verse 4 they had "left their first love." We might say that it is awful that they would do such a thing, shame on them. What about us? Do you remember when you first got saved. For many that is a "cloud nine" experience. We will never let anything interfere with our serving the Lord. We will always be a true and faithful follower. Backslide? No way. Then shortly after Goliath appears he begins doing all he can to distract us from demonstrating our love to the Lord as we should. Work, family, hobbies, being tired, etc. all begin to erode our staying close to the Lord and "following in His steps" as Peter emphasizes. D.L. Moody said, "I have never met a man who has given me as much trouble as myself." We often put it this way, "I'm my own worst enemy." John Newton (1725-1807), the Anglican minister who wrote Amazing Grace, said, "I am not the man I ought to be, I am not the man I wish to be and I am not the man I hope to be, but by the grace of God, I am not the man I used to be." I guess we are all diamonds in the rough, a work in progress.

What about Smyrna? (Revelation 2:9-11). What was their problem? Interestingly, the Smyrna church was not chastised or rebuked. In fact, the Lord praises them for being so faithful in the face of various kinds of persecution. If the Lord looks at our churches and we as individuals today, can He say the same about us? Faithfulness and obedience to God and His Word is expected, even commanded. Does He find us faithful now? Will He find us faithful when He comes to rapture His church, His Bride, the Body of Christ? Goliath tells us faithfulness is not necessary. It is another one of his lies. May we learn from the example of the church in Smyrna!

The Lord commends the church at Pergamos about some things but scolds them about some other things (Revelation 2:12-17). This church has become caught up in false doctrine and Jesus says he hates that. He instructs them to repent or face the consequences. The Bible says in Ephesians 4:14 (Paul's words to the church at Ephesus), "That we henceforth be no more children, tossed to and fro, and carried about with every wind of doctrine, by the sleight of men, and cunning craftiness, whereby they lie in wait to deceive." The New English Bible translation says it this way, "Then we shall no longer be children, carried about by the waves and blown about by every shifting wind of doctrine, led astray by the tricks of dishonest men." Paul also said in 1 Corinthians 13:11, "When I was a child, I spake as a child, I understood as a child, I thought as a child: but when I became a man, I put away childish things." Jesus expects us to grow up in our faith, to mature in our faith. That is what sanctification is all about. God has set us apart with a purpose. It's not a matter of just getting saved and then sitting on the sidelines waiting for the Lord to come and get us. The Lord has a purpose for every individual He creates and expects us to fulfill that purpose. The only way that is possible is through the operation of the Holy Spirit in our lives. To the church at Colosse Paul wrote (Colossians 2:6-7) "As ye have therefore received Christ Jesus the Lord, so walk ye in him. Rooted and built up in him, and stablished in the faith, as ye have been taught, abounding therein with thanksgiving." God is looking for faithful, obedient servants — who are walking with Him and who are rooted in the faith. It requires being filled with and walking in the Holy Spirit for that to happen? What about us? Can that be said of us? Can the Lord depend on us to carry out the purpose for which we have been created? The non-believers in our sinful world are destined for hell, unless we become a part of the rescue team. We can't save people but we can and should be telling them about the Savior who can. One night recently I went to dinner by myself in another town. Before I even arrived at the town (I had a doctor's appointment), I kept thinking of a particular restaurant. After my doctor's visit, I got in my vehicle and started toward the restaurant I had on my mind. Then, I thought no I will eat somewhere else. I drove to the other location but I realized I needed to go back to the restaurant I had on my mind. So, I did. A young lady was my waitress. She did a good job serving me and the meal was great. After I finished eating, I engaged in a conversation with her about my illnesses and how my faith had helped me through those maladies. She sat down across from me in the booth. I told her I didn't want to keep her because she had things to do. She began to share some of her own medical challenges (a couple of them could be life threatening). I continued to share my faith with her. I asked her if I could pray for her. She immediately said yes. We joined hands and I prayed. When I finished, she said it had made her day. There are times when I share the Lord with someone in Walmart or some other business. I am reminded of the information in the Bible that reveals Jesus' ministry is that it was mostly one on one. There are only a few examples of Him speaking to groups or crowds. May we never take for granted the opportunities the Lord puts in front of us. May we never forget that ministry "at church" is limited. The real ministry occurs in the marketplace. Several years ago, I heard an African American preacher at a convention. His name is Frederick G. Sampson. That day he made a very poignant observation. He said the "chores" are done around the house but the "work" is done in the fields. Jesus said in John 4:35, "Say not ye, There are yet four months, and then cometh harvest? Behold I say unto you, Lift up your eyes, and look on the fields; for they are white already to harvest." Oftentimes when people retire, they take care of things they did not have time for when they were working. That's not how the work of the kingdom works. Those who are lost are to be harvested now, not later.

The church at Thyatira is up next (Revelation 2:18-29). Basically, Jesus' problem with this church was their tolerance of Jezebel. This woman was the spouse of ole' King Ahab. He wasn't exactly a "goodie two shoes" himself (Baal worshiper, weak, spineless fella). He was a terrible king over Israel. Jezebel was full to the brim of Goliath (Satan). That evil spirit she had in her manifested itself in rejecting God and instead she was deep into worshiping Baal. She persecuted God's people, including his prophets. The name Jezebel to this day is associated with a spirit of evil. It is through people with a wicked spirit that Goliath revels. Don't let him win. We don't have to let him win. It's a choice. One of the things I include in my daily praying is, "Lord, help me to resist the devil and overcome evil with good." I also pray, "Father, help me to remember that the battle is yours and that no weapon will be used against me." Once again, this is where the wearing of the whole armor comes in.

Sardis takes the stage next (Revelation 3:1-6). The church at Sardis put up a good front but were "dead as a door nail." They were lethargic, lazy, not taking the Lord's work seriously. They were asleep on the job. Folks it is easy for any of us to be given to slumber. Because of my medical conditions and medications, I stay tired all the time. It's all I can do to get out of bed most days. There isn't a day that I feel well. This has now gone on for years. It is uncomfortable and discouraging. However, although limited in what I can now do, there are some things I refuse to neglect. I do daily devotions, and I attend church if I am at all up to it physically. I try to financially support my church, the cowboy church, and other charity organizations. I look for opportunities to witness when I am out an about. Although limited, I still preach when there is an invitation to do so. Writing this book is something I can do. My prayer is that it will help my readers. I say none of this braggingly but humbly. My point is that at our weakest we are able to do something for the Lord. He is telling the church at Sardis to wake up.

Now we'll look at the church at Philadelphia (Revelation 3:7-13). What were they up to? Well, lots of good stuff. He recognizes their faithfulness and service despite their lack of resources. There are circumstances with plenty of churches that don't have all the funds they need to do what they would like to do. There may be a reservoir of other needs they have. Regardless, they use what they do have to be a soul winning station. As individuals and families we may not possess all we would like to have yet the Lord meets our needs. Whatever our resources we need to serve the Lord and believe that our God "will supply all your need according to his riches in glory by Christ Jesus." (Phillipians 4:19). It is amazing what God can do with so little. In Mark 12 Jesus was watching rich people put lots of money in the treasury of the temple. Then he noticed a poor widow toss in her two mites (a pittance by most standards). Jesus took His disciples aside, as recorded in verses 12-13, He said to them, "Verily I say unto you, That this poor widow hath cast more in, than all they which have cast into the treasury. For all they did cast in of their abundance; but she of her want did cast in all that she had, even her living." She may have not known from where her next meal would come but she gave out of not the abundance of wealth but out of the abundance of her heart. In 1 Corinthians 9:7 Paul taught the Corinthian church this about giving, "Every man according as he purposeth in his heart, so let him give; not grudgingly, or of necessity: for God loveth a cheerful giver." The Lord is so reasonable. Malachi 3:10 says, "Bring ye all the tithes into the storehouse, that there may be meat in mine house, and prove me now herewith, saith the Lord of hosts, if I will not open you the windows of heaven, and pour you out a blessing, that there shall not be room to receive it." The Hebrew for tithe is maser, which simply means ten percent. Yes, God is so reasonable. We earn one hundred percent, we keep ninety percent, and we give Him ten percent. I can tell you that I have never regretted tithing. Even when I thought I needed it for other things, I tithed anyway. I have never suffered because of giving to the Lord. As a pastor in my home church used to say before the offering was received, "We believe the tithe belongs to the Lord, you make Him and offering." A number of years ago in one of my former pastorates I preached on tithing on a Sunday morning. Not long after that Sunday I saw one of our young married couples drive in the church parking lot with a new vehicle. I complimented the gentleman. He said, "That's okay, we can afford it." Then he proceeded to tell me that after that Sunday morning when I preached on tithing that he and his wife went home and prayerfully discussed the sermon. They had been giving to the church but had not been tithing. They made a commitment to tithe. Shortly after that he got an unexpected promotion at his work, and his wife also got an unexpected raise with her job and a position she had wanted. God is faithful and He keeps His promises!

Next up and the last of the seven churches of Asia Minor we will examine is the church at Laodicea (Revelation 3:14-22). For our purposes here I will quote verses 15-17, "I know thy works, that thou art neither cold nor hot: I would thou wert cold or hot. So then because thou art lukewarm, and neither cold nor hot: I will spue thee out of my mouth. Because thou sayest, I am rich, and increased with goods, and have need of nothing; and knowest not that thou art wretched, and miserable, and poor, and blind, and naked." These Laodiceans were full of themselves. They could not afford to not be committed to the Lord. They had their wealth. They had their material goods. They lived in an affluent town. The fact is that they were delusional. Who were they kidding? Who are we kidding if we depend on ourselves instead of God. We are helpless without Him. We are only able to breathe because of the life He placed in us while we were still in our mother's womb. He can stop that breathing whenever He chooses. A sidebar note here is that being fully committed, completely engaged, and on fire for our Lord is how we have joy and happiness as believers. Don't allow Goliath to steal your joy! After Jesus addresses the seven churches, I love the invitation and assurance he offers in Revelation 3:19-21, "Behold, I stand at the door and knock: if any man hear my voice, and open the door, I will come into him, and will sup (to dine with, and have a close and intimate fellowship) with him and he with me. To him that overcometh will I grant to sit with me in my throne, even as I also overcame, and am set down with my Father in his throne. He that hath an ear, let him hear what the Spirit saith unto the churches." If our practice in our faith is lukewarm it makes Jesus want to throw up. Do we want to make people here on earth that we love vomit? Of course not. Then why would we do that to our Lord of Lords and

King of kings?

Now that I have at least highlighted some information about the Church Age, we will examine the progression following that age, where we are now living, with the topics I will discuss of the Last Days, between the Church Age and the New Heaven and New Earth. Following is the outline that will be our guide (all Scripturally based).

THE RAPTURE
THE GREAT TRIBULATION
The Seven Seals
The Seven Trumpets
War in Heaven
The Seven Bowls
The Second Coming
The 1,000-Year Reign of Jesus Christ & All the Saints
The Great White Throne Judgment
The New Heaven and New Earth

After addressing these periods and events this chapter will be concluded.

The Seven Seals, Seven Trumpets, and Seven Bowls all describe the events of the Great Tribulation, a period of devastation, destruction, suffering, and death that are all beyond our imagination. It begins after the Rapture.

The Seven Seals

The 7 Seals are (1) White Horse; (2) Red Horse; (3) Black Horse; (4) Pale Horse; (5) Souls Under the Altar; (6) Whole World Trembles; (7) Silence.

Revelation 5:1-2, "And I saw in the right hand of him that sat on the throne a book written within and on the backside, sealed with seven seals. And I saw a strong angel proclaiming with a loud voice, Who is worthy to open the book, and to loose the seals thereof? Then, in verse 5 John writes, "And one of the elders saith unto me, Weep not: behold the Lion of the tribe of Juda, the Root of David, hath prevailed to open the book, and to loose the seven seals thereof.

Seal # 1: Revelation 6:2, "And I saw, and behold a white horse: and he that sat on him had a bow; and a crown was given unto him: and he went forth conquering, and to conquer. Bible scholars don't all agree on the interpretation of the white horse. Some see it as Jesus riding the white horse with His conquering power. Some believe it to be the church who is the rider, delivering the message of the Lord. The last view (and is the one held by most scholars) is that the rider is the antichrist and so to speak "appears as an angel of light." Someone who tries to impersonate Jesus in His purity, and he gains worldly power and dominance. Of course, this would be a false representation of our Blessed Savior.

Seal # 2: Revelation 6:4, "And there went out another horse that was red: and power was given to him that sat thereon to take peace from the earth, and that they should kill one another: and there was given unto him a great sword." This seal describes a bloody and devastating conflict that leads to collapse of society.

Seal # 3: Revelation 6:5-6, "And when he had opened the third seal, I heard the third beast say, Come and see. And I beheld, and lo a black horse; and he that sat on him had a pair of balances in his hand. And I heard a voice in the midst of the four beasts say, A measure of wheat for a penny, and three measures of barley for a penny; and see thou hurt not the oil and the wine." Here is described lack of food and severe hunger, a plummeting economy. Seems that the primary population that will be impacted are those who are poor.

Seal # 4: Revelation 6:7-8, "And when he opened the fourth seal, I heard the voice of the fourth beast say, Come and see. And I looked, and behold a pale horse: and his name that sat on him was Death. And Hell followed with him. And power was given unto them over the fourth part of the earth, to kill with the sword, and with hunger, and with death, and with the beasts of the earth." This reflects the judgment and anger of God on our earth. The results? A fourth part of the earth will experience unbelievable havoc and death.

Seal # 5: Revelation 6:9-11, "And when he had opened the fifth seal, I saw under the altar the souls of them that were slain for the Word of God, and for the testimony which they held: And they cried with a loud voice, saying How long, O Lord, holy and true, dost thou not judge and avenge our blood on them that dwell on the earth? And white robes were given unto every one of them; and it was said unto them, that they should rest yet for a little season, until their fellow servants also and their brethren, that should be killed as they were, should be fulfilled." Described here are the martyrs who died for the Lord. He asks them to be patient, there are more martyrs that will yet die. They are assured that the Lord will not forget them. He is telling them to stand by, the final victory is on its way. Incidentally, this Scripture lends itself to belief that those who have gone to be with the Lord are aware of at least some of the things which are going on here on earth. Many years ago, a black pastor invited me to a "7 Seal Service." He was inviting 7 pastors, with each one being assigned a different seal, to briefly speak on their designated seal. My assignment was this one on the martyrs.

Seal # 6: Revelation 6:12-17. Since there are several verses pertaining to this seal, I am just sharing verses 12 and 13. I will highlight the rest of the passage. Verses 12-13, "And I beheld when he had opened the sixth seal, and, lo, there was a great earthquake; and the sun became black as sackcloth of hair, and the moon became as blood; And the stars of heaven fell unto the earth, even as a fig tree casteth her untimely figs, when she is shaken as a mighty wind." We also learn that "heaven departed as a scroll," the mountains were moved, people of all stations and ranks hid in the rocks, they asked to be hidden from the Lord and the wrath that will be released. What a sad and frightening picture this passage portrays. It definitely pays to be prepared. Folks, the world will end and then the judgment. Are you ready?

Seal # 7: Revelation 8:1-7. I am providing verses 1 and 2 here, "And when he had opened the seventh seal, there was silence in heaven about the space of half an hour. And I saw the seven angels which stood before God; and to them were given seven trumpets." The silence here represents that which is to come, namely the judgments involved in the seven trumpets.

Please keep in mind that there is more information regarding the verses I haven't stated. Go back and read the entire passages, in fact, read the entire Book of Revelation for further enlightenment.

The Seven Trumpets
(Revelation 8-11:19)

The trumpets are designed by God to announce the forthcoming judgment, punishment, unbearable suffering. No one who understands what is coming in the Great Tribulation and is in their right mind wants to be here during this period. How do you miss it? Accept Jesus Christ as your Lord and Savior, because only believers will be raptured out prior to the Tribulation. The declaration is beyond our finite minds. The destruction and death are measured out mathematically, as in one-third, a tenth, etc. The bottom line is that all that is poured out is inconceivable. We're talking hail with blood, trees and grass burned up, sea turning to blood, sea creatures dying, ships destroyed, a great star falling into rivers and fountains of water, sun and moon affected so as not to give light in a large percentage of the earth, earthquake, billows of smoke rising from the bottomless pit, ugly and deadly locusts, people will be pleading to die but it won't happen—

they will stay around for the over the top suffering. I choose Jesus! I choose to be in the rapture! What about you? We all have a choice but it must be made in time. When is that? Well, that's just it, could be awhile or in the next minute.

During the Great Tribulation the dragon, the beast who is the anti-Christ, and the false prophet will be right in the middle of all the events during this period.

The Seven Bowls
(Revelation 15:5-8)

Now we have seven angels who have seven bowls, full of what no human being wants to encounter. Verses 6-7, "And the seven angels came out of the temple, having the seven plagues, clothed in pure and white linen, and having their breasts girded with golden girdles. And one of the four beasts gave unto the seven angels seven golden vials full of the wrath of God, who liveth forever and ever." Again, this is the final blow by God. We can be certain that this would be akin to what some would describe "as all hell breaking loose." It is the unthinkable punishment that no one wants to experience.

We know from Scripture that the first three and a half years of the Great Tribulation will be somewhat peaceful. The anti-Christ will deceive the masses. He will seem like "the best thing since sliced bread." Then, the hammer falls. He will declare himself God and those who do not agree to take the mark of the beast are in for it. Do not, and again I say do not wait, hoping you will have some chance during the tribulation. Who trades being with Jesus in Paradise for the indescribable suffering of the Tribulation?

Okay, the Tribulation concludes. While controversial, some believe there will be another opportunity during that period to accept the Lord—especially Jews who rejected Christ as the Messiah. Some verses that prompt people to believe that there will be another chance to accept the Lord in the Tribulation period are: Jeremiah 30:7, "...for that day is great, so that none is like it: it is even the time of Jacob's trouble; but he shall be saved out of it." Romans 11:26-27, "And so all Israel shall be saved: as it is written, There shall come out of Sion the Deliverer, and shall turn away ungodliness from Jacob: For this is my covenant unto them, when I shall take away their sins." Revelation 7:4, "And I heard the number of them which were sealed: and there were sealed an hundred and forty and four thousand of all the tribes of the children of Israel." Revelation 7:13-14, "And one of the elders answered, saying unto me, What are these which are arrayed in white robes? And whence came they? And I said unto him, Sir, thou knowest. And he said to me, These are they which came out of great tribulation, and have washed their robes, and made them white in the blood of the Lamb." While many reputable Bible scholars subscribe to people being saved during the Tribulation, I leave it to you my readers, based on Scripture, to draw your own conclusion. Maybe it is similar to the Garden of Eden. God intended this earth to last forever, until sin destroyed that plan. In the New Jerusalem God will still have His way. Satan won't be around to mess it up, so we can be confident that when the Lord brings down the New Jerusalem to this earth, His original plan will be accomplished. The Jews have rejected Jesus as their Messiah. Maybe the Lord will make a special provision for "His own that received Him not" (John 1:11) but will in the finality see Him for who He is and accept Him. I am only talking about those who will accept Him, not those who have died without Jesus—Jew or Gentile. The Bible makes it clear in several places that no one enters Heaven except through our Lord Jesus Christ.

The Rapture
There is not total agreement about the Rapture.

Some don't believe that will happen. Others do. I strongly believe in the Rapture because there is biblical evidence to support such an event. There are those who believe that we go straight from the Tribulation to the Second Coming, and that the church will be here during the Great Tribulation. I believe that the Rapture and the Second Coming are two separate events on God's calendar.

It is true that the word rapture is not in the Bible. Then where do we get that there is such an event? While rapture is not in the Bible, it is a word that has gained usage because of what the Bible does say (which I will mention in a bit). The Latin word for rapture is *rapturo*. The Latin meaning is a snatching away or a carrying off. Now, let's examine some supporting Bible passages. I think the primary Scripture is found in 1 Thessalonians 4:16-17. This verse I have used numerous times in conducting funerals, especially at the gravesite. This is what the Apostle Paul says in those verses, "For the Lord himself will descend from heaven with a shout, with the voice of the archangel, and with the trump of God: and the dead in Christ shall rise first: Then we which are alive and remain shall be caught up together with them in the clouds, to meet the Lord in the air: and so shall we ever be with the Lord." Matthew 24:39-41 records Jesus' words, "...so shall also the coming the Son of man be. Then shall two be in the field; the one shall be taken, and the other left. Two women shall be grinding at the mill; the one shall be taken, and the other left." To me, it's clear that with those not taken still being here on earth, those taken will be separated to another location. I believe that is Paradise, or what we sometimes call the intermediate Heaven. When Jesus descends the next time, it will be His Second Coming. He won't be taking one and leaving one. He will be returning with His army, all His saints to rule with Him in the 1,000-year reign. Following the Rapture of the church, the body of Christ, His bride, the Marriage Supper of the Lamb, the Judgment Seat of Christ for Christians to answer what we have done and be rewarded accordingly will occur. This judgment is not for salvation. That comes only by grace through faith. As I said before, none of us could possibly do enough to earn our way to Heaven. Speaking of rewards, here are some passages for your consideration. 1 Corinthians 3:23-15, "Every man's work shall be manifest: for the day shall declare it, because it shall be revealed by fire; and the fire shall try every man's work of what sort it is. If any man's work abide which he hath built thereupon, he shall receive a reward. If any man's work shall be burned, he shall suffer loss: but he himself shall be saved; yet so as by fire." 1 Corinthians 5:10, "For we must all (believers) appear before the judgment seat of Christ; that everyone may receive the things done in his body, according to that he hath done, whether it be good or bad." Remember, Paul is writing these two letters to Christians in the church at Corinth. This is not the same judgment as the Great White Throne Judgment, which is reserved for those who die without Christ. The Great White Throne Judgment occurs after the Millennium (the thousand-year reign). The Battle of Armageddon occurs before the Millennium. First, we will look at the thousand-year period and I will touch on Armageddon afterwards.

Remember, during the rapture Jesus meets believers in the air. At His second coming following the tribulation and initiating the thousand-year reign, he sets foot on the Mt. of Olives, from where He was ascended.

The Second Coming
(Jesus returns to Jerusalem on the Mount of Olives bringing His Bride with Him)

The Millennium
(1,000 Year Reign)
Christ returns! Hallelujah! Although relative

peace, this period will be like no other. Satan will be bound for the entire thousand years. Things will not be perfect but closer to that than anything we have known before on the earth. If you believe that people will be saved during the tribulation (all who could survive such horrors), then they will be alive during this period God has planned. So, they would not have yet gone to Paradise, and they would not have glorified bodies. Therefore, though they would love the Lord and would be committed to serving Him, they would not be perfect. However, this period will be a beautiful experience — in the abstract — God's schematic.

Old Testament prophets, such as Isaiah and Ezekiel, weigh in prophetically relative to this period. Of course, Revelation provides information. As I already mentioned, it is hands off for Satan. As prophesied, Jesus as a descendant of David will reign and rule from Jerusalem. Yes, Israel is a pivotal point for this age. Imagine peace and folks getting along like never before. Obviously, people will likely live longer but some think death will happen possibly to those saved during the millennium, and the time for that would not necessarily be in a thousand years. Wildlife will be compatible. That's a "game" changer.

A Note About Armageddon

Before the thousand years, Satan garners all the help he can find from other nations for one last battle (the Battle of Armageddon) where he is handily defeated by King Jesus and His forces. Armageddon is mentioned in Revelation 16:16. Location of the battle is in Megiddo in Israel in the Jezreel Valley. Several years ago, I stood on Mt. Carmel overlooking the Jezreel Valley. As I was looking over the battlefield, two Israeli military jets flew over. The whole experience was surreal for me. Mt. Carmel is also the location where the prophet Elijah called down fire from Heaven to prove to the prophets of Baal that God is for real. Of course, Goliath (Satan) is handily defeated. Time for him to go to jail for a thousand years. When his sentence is finished it is just really beginning. He will be in the lake of fire for eternity. In fact, the whole bunch will be sent there—Satan and his demons, fallen angels, all of his cohorts, and everyone who has rejected the Lord Jesus.

The Great White Throne Judgment
(Revelation 20:11-15)

"And I saw a great white throne, and him that sat on it, from whose face the earth and the heaven fled away; and there was found no place for them.

And I saw the dead, small and great, stand before God; and the books were opened: and another book was opened, which is the book of life: and the dead were judged out of those things which were written in the books, according to their works. And the sea gave up the dead which were in it; and death and hell delivered up the dead which were in them: and they were judged every man according to their works. And death and hell were cast into the lake of fire. This is the second death. And whosoever was not found written in the book of life was cast into the lake of fire."

This judgment, this eternal (second) death does not paint a pretty picture. What is recorded in the Bible is not a work of fiction, it is not a fake, it is not a fabrication, it is not a fairy tale — it is as real as it gets. There are no tough guys in hell. Because my wife knew that I was all about protecting my family, and others if I had the opportunity (of course I had to make that decision before I ever put a badge on in law enforcement), and that I had trained not only in law enforcement but martial arts, and that I wore boots, drove a pickup, and never got far from my firearms *LOL* –she saw me as what she called a "scrapper." Truth is that I have spent my whole life trying to help and minister to people. I love people and I care about people. I have never wanted to harm someone, and I am certainly not "trigger happy." Admittedly I do believe in the right to protect oneself, his family, and others. While not to an extreme, I am a bit of a survivalist, a prepper. Back in the day I wasn't a very large person, although at my peak I was 5'10" and 185. Now? Well, I am 80 years old, 5'7" and 125. Yep, no more fighting for this guy. I stay close to my weaponry. More importantly, while I believe God helps those who help themselves and He gave us a brain to use, I mostly depend on my faith in Him to watch over me. One thing you can be sure of, I am not tough enough to handle hell and shudder at the thought of having to go there. Thank you, Lord for saving my soul—that which lives with You forever. The greatest dispatching of Goliath is done by accepting Jesus as our Savior trusting what He did for us on the cross, and seeking His forgiveness.

The New Heaven and The New Earth

After everything has occurred during the last days the New Heaven & the New Earth will happen. This will be the final place for all believers. It is what every Christian has anticipated since their salvation experience. For those of us who are realists we know our time on earth, no matter how long it may be, is short. Let's say we live to be a hundred (and only a few do), that's no time at all when compared to eternity. Goliath does everything in his power to persuade us to invest everything in our earthly experience and not give attention to forever. It is just something else he lies about.

I do hope we understand the Lord is coming back for His people, His church, His bride — not for denominations. He created the church. We are the ones who have divided ourselves into separate groups. I sometimes think the Lord must be shaking His head because the divisions are not what he founded or intended. While I have a certain sense of loyalty to my denomination and to my local church, I pray that I will never allow that loyalty to see others as wrong and me as right. I strongly suspect that when we get to "the other side" we will be surprised theologically, doctrinally. Since we have all the many denominations, I hope that we respect the differences that may exist. I am not suggesting that we agree or endorse something that we understand to be anti-biblical. It is sort of a matter of agreeing to disagree and loving everyone. Over the years I have met some people that won't be happy if it is not just their group there. What will happen? Will they refuse to enter Heaven? The Lord is not returning to load up Baptists, Pentecostals,

Presbyterians, Nazarenes, Christian Churches, Church of Christ, Church of God, Methodists, Episcopalians, Catholics, Congregationalists, Friends Churches, Non-Denominational Churches, and the list is endless. While it is controversial, don't be too quick to judge those who emphasize healing, infilling of the Holy Spirit, exercise of the gifts of the Spirit. God works in each of us as sees fit. Because we might not all have the same experience with the Holy Spirit, doesn't make another's experience counterfeit. Criticizing, judging, or condemning can be dangerous.

So, all the last events in God's plan for the wrap up here on earth are finished. His final touch is our final landing place. We are talking about an indescribable splendor. Nothing will ever taint our eternal home. Just think, no more suffering, sickness, pain, sorrow, tears, darkness, death. It also means no more Goliath, evil, and sin. There is a beautiful prophetic passage in Isaiah 65:17-25 that describes this final place of joy. He says, in verse 17, "For, behold, I create new heavens and a new earth: and the former shall not be remembered, nor come to mind." Isaiah is not saying we will remember nothing but all the bad that has happened in the past will be erased. In 1 Peter 3:10-12, Peter explains that when the Lord returns there will be a great and fervent fire. The fire will burn what has been and create an environment of a New Heaven and a New Earth. Revelation 21:1-4 gives us a clear picture of what to expect in our new home, "And I saw a new heaven and a new earth: for the first heaven and the first earth were passed away; and there was no more sea. And I John saw the holy city, new Jerusalem, coming down from God out of heaven, prepared as a bride adorned for her husband. And I heard a great voice out of heaven, Behold, the tabernacle of God is with men, and he will dwell with them, and they shall be his people, and God himself shall be with them, and be their God. And God shall wipe away all tears from their eyes; and there shall be no more death, neither sorrow, nor crying, neither shall there be anymore pain: for the former things are passed away." Praise God, what a golden promise to every believer!

I love 1 Corinthians 2:9, "But as it is written, Eye hath not seen, nor ear heard, neither have entered into the heart of man, the things which God hath prepared for them that love him." No matter how hard we try we simply cannot grasp God's power, nor His wisdom. From the experience of salvation all the way to the New Jerusalem, we cannot fully comprehend all He has done to reveal His love to us and rescue us. I get excited just writing about this subject. Physically I no longer see or hear very well. Spiritually my ability to completely understand and appreciate all God has done, is doing, and will do is limited. I do see and hear enough from His Word and His Spirit to know that it is wonderful, and so is He.

When I think about all God has prepared for us, I think first and foremost about being with Jesus — just to be in His presence and worship our King! Next, I think about the blessed reunion with my family — my Carol, our kids and grandkids (and all their spouses), my great grandkids, my parents, my siblings, my sisters-in-law, my brothers-in-law, my aunts and uncles, my nephews and nieces, my cousins, my friends and acquaintances, and the folks I am yet to meet. Of course, while some are already with the Lord, some of us are still here. John Bunyan, the 17th century English writer and preacher (renown as the writer of Pilgrim's Progress) once said, "Death is but a portal out of a prison to a palace."

Robert Frost, the 20th century American poet is best known for his poem "The Road Not Taken." Here are the last 3 lines of that poem.

Two roads diverged in a wood, and I—

I took the one less traveled by,
And that has made all the difference.

Jesus said something similar about eternal life. There are two roads from which to choose. Will we choose the right one? Listen to Jesus' words as recorded in Matthew 7:13-14, "Enter ye in at the strait gate: for wide is the gate, and broad is the way, that leadeth to destruction, and many there be which go in thereat: Because strait is the gate, and narrow is the way, which leadeth unto life, and few there be that find it." We need to choose the road less traveled. Unbelievers may mock us, make fun of us and even ridicule us — but they are on the road to perdition. Don't forget that. In Isaiah 45:22-23, the Lord is speaking and says this, "Look unto me, and be ye saved, all the ends of the earth: for I am God, and there is none else. I have sworn by myself, the word has gone out of my mouth in righteousness, and shall not return, That unto me every knee shall bow, every tongue shall swear." Revelation 2:10-11 says something similar. People, you can do that now or later. Problem is that later is too late.

Since this life is temporary, the brevity alone should make us desire this New Heaven and the New Earth. Yes, we may go through a lot before we leave this earth. I know. I have had more than my share of grief and sickness — but oh what awaits us if Jesus is holding our hand.

If you aren't ready, you are on the most traveled road (which most people are). That route can be altered instantly. Just ask the Lord to forgive you of your sins, believe in what Jesus did on the cross for you, and accept Him as your Savior. It isn't complicated. He made the plan of salvation so simple that even children can understand it. It is not only a matter of Goliath being dispatched but a matter of you losing.

Chapter 12
Make Sure Goliath Loses

This chapter was co-Authored by Carol Lorraine Owens Bryant

I mentioned in an earlier chapter that Carol had thought about writing a book. We also discussed our jointly writing a book. That didn't happen and it won't happen now. However, as a tribute to her and her memory, you will also hear from her posthumously in this last chapter.

1 Corinthians 15:24-26 says, "Then cometh the end, when he shall have delivered up the kingdom to God, even the Father; when he shall have put down all rule and all authority and power. For he must reign, till he hath put all enemies under his

feet. The last enemy that shall be destroyed is death." I am thrilled by the fact that Carol and my family who have died in the Lord have already had death destroyed for them. There are three major things that keep me going here on earth at this point. First, is that I know the Lord left me here for a purpose and I want to fulfill that purpose until He takes me home. Second is being here for my family. As I shared in an earlier chapter, it is a large family—consisting of two daughters, two sons, twelve grandkids, and two great grandkids. Then of course there are the spouses, four of our kids, and five of our grandkids (so far). It was devastating for our kids and for me to lose their mom. She really was the central person for all of us. As this last chapter is being written, she has been gone a little over two and a half years. I have been through much in my life but losing her is the most difficult thing of all. There are no words. I live on memories, her pictures, my trips to the cemetery. The third thing that keeps me going is the promise of me being reunited with Carol, other family and friends. I know it will be in a different but much higher way that will bring complete joy.

As I think about my own death (I know that's morbid) but it is where I am in my journey. I have made some requests for my funeral service. Among those are three songs I would like to have sung. One is "Through It All" as I mentioned earlier, written by Andrae' Crouch; another one is "Rise Again," written by Dallas Holm; and the third one is "Here We Are," written also by Dallas Holm. These songs express my own faith journey and my belief that Jesus *is* coming back for His church.

He rose again and so will His believers. He is coming back for us.

God the Father, Jesus the Son, and the Holy Spirit all deserve our praise, our adoration, our worship, our all in all.

I want those to be my last messages to the people who will grieve at my passing.

Among songs of the fifties, sixties, seventies, etc. there are some that speak to me about my relationship with Carol. Some of those are "Unchained Melody," "Crying," "The Rose," "Love in the First Degree," "Endless Love," and "Goodbye" (Kenny Rogers). In a way they exacerbate my grief, yet in another way they remind me of when we were young and enjoyed songs with a romantic flare. From when we met as young teenagers, till now, I have always loved my soulmate. She was my life, my everything. The happiness that I found in her can never be the same without her. I am so thankful for God's promise, Psalm 30:5, "...weeping may endure for a night, but joy cometh in the morning."

What really happens when we die? Angels transport our soul to Paradise (Luke 16:220). After breathing our last breath, we are instantly with the Lord (2 Corinthians 5:6). We are aware and our emotions are functional, and we have our memory (Luke 16:19-31). We know from chapters 4 and 5 in Revelation that we will be worshiping. Who knows what else the Lord will have us doing? It will all be wonderful. To some extent we may be aware of some things that are going on here on earth (Revelation 6:9-10). What about recognition? According to Matthew 17:1-3; Luke 16; 1 Thessalonians 4:13-18, it is more than implied. It tells us not to sorrow because God will bring them with Him, and they will greet us. 1 Corinthians 13:12 tells us that what we know about God and what we know of our loved ones who have gone on is limited but that will change when we get there. Now we "know in part." Once there, we will know each other on a much higher plane. Isaiah 55:8-9 explains, "For my thoughts are not your thoughts, neither are your ways my ways, saith the Lord. For as the heavens are higher than the earth, so are my ways higher than your ways, and my thoughts than your thoughts."

I have mentioned angels in this writing. I am not

including a study here of their role and their ministry in both the Old and New Testaments. They do have a needed, effective, magnificent service in the work of the Lord. I have taught about angels. At one time, Billy Graham published a book he wrote on the subject. Many other books have been written as well about angels. They are clearly ministering and watching over us.

This is the last chapter in this book, and Carol will conclude the chapter, posthumously. Following her graduation, her promotion to Heaven, we discovered some notes she had written in longhand. Although her life is her legacy, I want to show something tangible that reveals her heart and her relationship with the Lord. So, the following are some things she jotted down and were in her Bible.

From My Sweetheart Carol

These few notes were written by her several years ago, 1994 & 1995

"Keep us in your care Father. We are at your disposal. Surprise us, command us, use us as you will. Most of all, fill us with your Spirit. We are helpless. Wrap us in your warm robes of comfort and hold us together when we feel the world pulling us apart, abusing us. Give us your courage and battle savvy. We fight against unseen enemies — unrecognizable because we accept too much from Satan."

"I am more unsettled and confused about the demonstration (or lack of) worship than ever. Where are hearts, and souls, and minds when singing 'Love Lifted Me'; 'Jesus Paid It All'; 'Have Thine Own Way Lord'? How can those words flow from hollow mouths and hearts of mud? I'd like to shake us all until we learn to Praise the Lord – with cymbals, trumpets, lifting holy hands, shouts of joy."

"Behold the Lamb of God who takes away the sin of the world. Behold the Lamb who is slain. Behold the Lamb of God who takes away the sin of Carol. BEHOLD THE LAMB! Thank you, Jesus – You became poor to make me rich."

"What can wash away my sins? Nothing but the blood of Jesus. BEHOLD THE LAMB! I am ready for the spectacular sights, land of no nights, and the haven of rest, and the grandest of all – The Son of God."

Carol's thoughts are still timely for today. Do we spend enough time (any time) praising the Lord? God loves our praise of Him. He inhabits our praises, just as He did those of Israel (Psalm 22:3).

Conclusion

I hope that you have found this writing both comforting and challenging. My purpose in this writing is to do as the adage says about a preacher's mission, which is "to comfort the afflicted and afflict the comfortable." We live in a very cruel, evil, wicked world. In fact, as concerned as I am about the nuclear commination that exists, and the menacing and angry threats by such countries as Iran, Iraq, Afghanistan, China, Russia, North Korea, and others, I know beyond any doubt that the real battle/the war is the one between good and evil. It's a world filled with greed, selfishness, and sinful pride. My prayer is that those of you who are believers will find encouragement to "keep on keeping on." It is not easy, but no assignment is more important than for you and for me to serve our gracious God. This is a time in our journey where we are facing exigent demands relative to our time and to our priorities. Do not despair. Yes, Goliath is running around like crazy to distract and devour us. Remember, his mission is to "steal, kill, and destroy." (John 10:10) The good news is that we don't have to let him win. As we keep faith, he is a defeated foe. We must keep him under our feet. We can't do this Christian life without the one who invented Christianity. The Psalmist assures us of the Lord's presence, Psalm 121:1-4, "I will lift up mine eyes to the hills, from whence cometh my help. My help cometh from the Lord, which made heaven and earth. He will not suffer thy foot to be moved: he that keepeth thee will not slumber. Behold, he that keepeth Israel will neither slumber nor sleep." This is a promise to Israel. What about us? Once we are born again, we are the new Israel. Every Jew and every gentile who accept Jesus will enjoy the same Heaven. Galatians 3:26, 28, 29, "For ye are all the children of God by faith in Christ Jesus. There is neither Jew nor Greek, there is neither bond nor free, there is neither male nor female: for ye are all one in Christ Jesus. And if ye be Christ's, then ye are Abraham's seed, and heirs according to the promise." What is our mandate from the Lord? I think Paul answers that question in Phillipians 4:6-8, "...in everything by prayer and supplication with thanksgiving let your requests be made known unto God. And the peace of God, which passeth all understanding, shall keep your hearts and minds through Christ Jesus. Finally, brethren, whatsoever things are true, whatsoever things are honest, whatsoever things are just, whatsoever things are pure, whatsoever things are lovely, whatsoever things are of good report; if there be any virtue, and if there be any praise, think on these things." Time after time after time the Bible provides our marching orders. If you are reading this and you don't know Jesus, it is my prayer and heart's desire that you receive Him as your Savior. We all live the proverbial one heartbeat and one breath away from leaving this world. Now, you have a choice, be raptured or punished. If you don't know our Blessed Savior, Romans 10:9, 10, 13 tells us how to be saved, "That if thou shalt confess with thy mouth the Lord Jesus, and shalt believe in thy heart that God hath raised him from the dead, thou shalt be saved. For with the heart man believeth unto righteousness; and with the mouth confession is made unto salvation. For whosoever shall call upon the name of the Lord shall be saved." Then, affiliate yourself with a Bible believing church and follow the Lord in believer's baptism. Some things I have stated in this book may be hard for some to swallow. My "calling" is to proclaim the truth. Why? Because the truth will set you free (John 8:32). My focus in this writing has been to tell the truth, convey my love to you, and share the gospel with you. While the work is not intended to be a full autobiography, it is I suppose a "semi-autobiography." I am not important enough, or interesting enough to write and publish my memoirs. The personal illustrations are to help bring to light significant biblical truths. In sharing what the Holy Spirit has led me to share, I know I will likely look back on the finished project with frustration. I am confident that I will realize later that I should have included some information that I forgot. My fault, not His!

About the Author

Dr. Michael Wayne Bryant, Sr. has been in the ministry for sixty years. He received his undergraduate degree from the University of the Cumberlands (then Cumberland College) as well as receiving graduate degrees from International Seminary (BA, Th.M, D.Min). He has served as an associate pastor, senior pastor, evangelist, chaplain. He pastored several churches, and has done mission work in Washington DC, Mexico and Guatemala. Dr. Bryant has also served in more than a hundred religious, civic, charitable, and other community organizations. He is the recipient of several awards and has received honorable mention in various publications. In addition to serving with the Sheriff's Department for thirteen years, he was elected as Mayor of Mt. Vernon, KY three times and occupied that position for twelve years. He and his late wife Carol were married for fifty-seven years before her passing. He is the proud father of two daughters, Melissa and Marla, two sons, Michael and Matthew, twelve grandkids, a great grandson, and a great granddaughter (so far). Between his kids and grandkids there have been additions to the family with 9 spouses (so far). Dispatching Goliath was birthed out of prayer and the leadership of the Holy Spirit. May God bless His Word, which "shall not return unto me void" (Isaiah 55:11).